Anna

Anna

A Daughter's Life

WILLIAM LOIZEAUX

Arcade Publishing • New York

First Edition

Excerpt from *Letters to a Young Poet* by Rainer Maria Rilke, translated by M. D. Herter Norton, reprinted by permission of W. W. Norton & Company, Inc., © 1934 by W. W. Norton & Company, Inc., renewed 1962 by M. D. Herter Norton; revised edition © 1954 by W. W. Norton & Company, Inc., renewed 1982 by M. D. Herter Norton. Excerpt from "An Observation" by May Sarton from *As Does New Hampshire*, reprinted by kind permission of William L. Bauhan, publisher. Excerpts from "Home Burial" and "The Hill Wife" by Robert Frost, reprinted from *The Poetry of Robert Frost*, edited by Edward Connery Lathem, © 1916, 1930, 1939, 1969 by Holt, Rinehart and Winston, © 1944, 1958 by Robert Frost, © 1967 by Lesley Frost Ballantine; Henry Holt and Company, Inc., publisher. Epigraph to "Heart's Needle," by W. D. Snodgrass, reprinted by permission of Random House, Inc., © 1959, renewed 1983.

Library of Congress Cataloging-in-Publication Data
Loizeaux, William.
Anna : a daughter's life / by William Loizeaux.
p.   cm.
ISBN 1-55970-197-8 (hc)
ISBN 1-55970-231-1 (pb)
1. Loizeaux, Anna.   2. VATER syndrome — Patients — Biography.
I. Title.
RJ255.L65L65   1993
362.1'9892'0043092 — dc20
[B]   92-54256

Published by Arcade Publishing, Inc., New York

Distributed by Little, Brown and Company

10   9   8   7   6   5   4   3   2   1

Printed in the United States of America

For Beth

Acknowledgments

Many people have contributed to the writing of this book through their interest, encouragement, and sustaining friendship. Among them are John Auchard, Norma Tilden, Bonnie Bernstein, Hank Dobin, Ivy Goodman, Bob Levine, Joan Goldberg, Ted Leinwand, Rose Ann Fraistat, and Neil Fraistat. All, in their own ways, have enriched these pages. I am fortunate to have friends of such generous sympathy and passionate intelligence.

I'd particularly like to thank Howard Norman, Ivy Goodman, and Norma Tilden for their readings and rereadings of my manuscript, their detailed analyses and useful suggestions, their soft suasions toward reason.

To the staff at Arcade Publishing: I thank you all for your commitment to the spirit of this book. I cannot imagine working with better editors than Tim Bent, Jeannette Seaver, and Richard Seaver. In difficult times, they have taken great care.

Then finally, at the heart, there is Beth. Without her love, none of this would have been possible — none of it at all. That is why this book is dedicated to her. And to the memory of Anna.

You are my daughter still.

A Note to the Text

What follows is a journal I began some weeks after the death of our daughter, Anna. It is, above all, a memoir of her brief life and a year-long record of the lives she left behind. It is as truthful as my memory and imagination have allowed. And if there is any good in it, then I am happy for that, though such goodness is not, and never can be, worth its terrible cost.

I came to write this journal simply because I had to. There was no choice for me. I am a writer, and something had happened that I could not avoid, submerge, or somehow write *around*. It was with me every day. So every day I sat at my desk, wrote the date at the top of a page, and tried to fill the space beneath with what I was remembering, thinking, and feeling. I recall a wild need to set things down, to grasp with words what had gone from my hands, though the words seemed — they still seem — so inadequate. I needed to say that Anna was here, that this, however short, was a human life, and like all of our lives, any life, this deserves our attention.

There is a passage in Thoreau's *Walden* that I have always loved, and never so much as now.

I went to the woods because I wished to live deliberately, to front only the essential facts of life, and see if I could not learn what it had to teach, and not, when I came to die, discover that I had not lived. I did not wish to live what was not life, living is so dear; nor did I wish to practise resignation, unless it was quite necessary. I wanted to live deep and suck out all the marrow of life, to live so sturdily and Spartan-like as to put to rout all that was not life, to cut a broad swath and shave close, to drive life into a corner, and reduce it to its lowest terms, and, if it proved to be mean, why then to get the whole and genuine meanness of it, and publish its meanness to the world; or if it were sublime, to know it by experience, and be able to give a true account of it in my next excursion.

Anna took my wife, Beth, and me to the woods, to a place we would have done anything to avoid, a place where we never would have gone on our own, where we had to live deliberately, day to day, and face the more essential facts of our lives. Because of Anna, I have come to know better what is mean, what is random, devastating, and what, by force of friendship and love, is sublime. I have seen my daughter born, live, and die. I have been awed by her joy, strength, infant courage, by her mother's fierce devotion, and by the hands, often strangers' hands, that reached to comfort and know her. I have been heartbroken by her pain and death, and awed anew by those who still reach out and remember.

I can offer no prescription for dealing with the losses that we all inevitably face, except to live them and share them as fully as we can. I see no road maps to easy comfort and acceptance. The best I can do is be true to the experience, or as near as my words can come. I can tell the story, Anna's story, and try to share the wonder of her life and the intractable mystery of her death. The words are mine, but the story is hers. If I have grown in the living or grown in the telling — or if anyone can grow in the reading of this — then that is Anna's gift.

W.L.
Hyattsville, Maryland

x

Anna

August 21, 1989
HYATTSVILLE, MARYLAND

On January 21, 1989, our first child, a daughter, Anna, was born. Five months and thirteen days later, on the morning of July 4, she died. During that time a small life was lived. And during that time my wife, Beth, and I were more alive than we ever have been — more alive with pain, sadness, fear, joy, hope, and despair.

Now it is seven weeks since the Fourth of July, and it is the day when Anna would have been seven months old. We have visited our families in Minnesota and New Jersey. We have hiked in the clean, clear air of the Adirondacks, swum in cold water where you can see straight to the sandy bottom. But today we are home in our asbestos-sided 1930s bungalow, where my study is still half-painted, where the water still drips in the sink upstairs, where cicadas churr in the oaks outside, where it has just rained, the air sweltering, air conditioners buzzing — another summer in metro D.C. — and where Anna's things are still scattered about: the four-legged Swyngomatic, a basket of toys in the dining room, the Wiggleworm, and on the floors, if you look closely, here and there her grainy splashes of dried spit-up. We haven't had the heart, yet, to change a thing. It all looks the same.

Though if you were to walk through these rooms, you would sense in the air that something has happened here, something with

3

such a residue of silence, sadness, and remembered joy. You would sense that nothing here is as it should have been.

So we walk through these rooms with aimless questions. Where is she now? Why? What reason? Why can't we hold her? Why isn't she asleep in the crib upstairs? When will she return? (another stay in the hospital?) — though of course there is the small blue box of ashes, a cup's worth, heavy, like a strange paperweight, on my bedroom bureau.

How can this be? How can any of this have really happened? And now I wonder, Should I write about this? Should I sit in the mornings and try to remember her, bring it all back, every detail: her long thumbs, her crazy hair, and the way she lay in a hospital crib for her last week — transformed, unconscious, though still alive, still her, still hearing our voices through the sedation, and squeezing our fingers, hard? Should I go over and over what shouldn't have been? Should I keep looking at what, in the end, is so unbearable?

I'm not sure. But is there really an alternative? For here was a life. Anna. A pure thing in a bare hand. To write her name is a painful comfort. It holds close what I can't let go, and what I can't forget.

There is nothing in this life without a marker.

August 22

When I came downstairs this morning to let out the dog, I saw that Beth had clipped a picture of Anna on our refrigerator door, alongside the grocery list and postcards there. In the photo, taken on the morning of June 27, the day she was admitted to the hospital for her heart surgery, Anna is looking straight into the camera — or straight at me right now as I look at an identical photograph on my desk before me. Anna's eyes are huge, dark, the flash of the camera in the points of her pupils. Her eyebrows are light brown, her lashes long. Her nose is small and rounded, her mouth slightly open, not exactly smiling, but she seems to be surprised by the flash, on the edge of delight, or on the edge of one of her bubbling sounds. Cooing.

4

She was at that stage. In the mornings she would babble for a half hour at a time, sometimes even before we were out of bed. We'd just lie there and listen, and she'd go on and on in her room around the corner, as if the whole world were nothing but sunlight in a dormer window. As if nothing in the world could change any of this.

How can I explain what it feels like for a sound to be gone? When each morning comes with birds and light and rustling traffic. When the newspaper thuds on the front porch step. When we get up without hearing, and go downstairs.

August 23

I was describing the photo. And I have said nothing about Anna's hair, which was simply wild, strands of it going this way and that, hanging over her ears, over one eyebrow or another. In the mornings it looked as if she had spent the night in a swirling windstorm, a child brought in from outdoors, all sleeked and tangled with oil or rain or dew or sweat. Her hair was turning brownish blonde at the time, a little darker than mine. When she was born it was jet black, and it was the first thing I saw as the doctor gracefully lifted Anna from the incision in Beth's stomach, turning her toward me with his hand behind her neck.

And there was all that hair. Black as a mink's, slick and gleaming beneath the big domed light. "She is beautiful," I remember saying to Beth, whose face was behind the blood-speckled screen. "She is beautiful." And after they had clipped the cord, suctioned her throat and lungs, and finished a quick exam, I remember the nurse laying Anna on the pillow beside Beth's shoulder. I remember Beth touching her carefully; Anna's bright red skin, her small fists clenched and toes curled in. I remember seeing their heads together, their hair identically black, identically messed, matted, wild — Beth and Anna — as if they had been out in the wind together.

That was on January 21, at 2:20 P.M. I have no idea what the weather was like or if anything else happened in the world that day. Anna was six pounds, two ounces. She had black hair and huge eyes.

5

She was all alive, all there, though as we would soon find out, she was not altogether well.

August 24

I have been reading Rilke's *Letters to a Young Poet*, and last night I came upon that passage where he writes, "We know little, but that we must hold to what is difficult . . . that something is difficult must be a reason the more for us to do it."

Now I am not exactly young, nor a poet, but reading this fills me with strange hope. Loss is difficult. Sadness is difficult. To remember is difficult. I hope from all of this that something can come, something maybe not whole or expressible, but true.

One of the sad things about losing Anna is that we will never be able to tell her (it would have been at some appropriate time) how strange, hard, and even humorous it was to conceive her. I don't remember the exact day it happened — it must have been about mid-May — but that doesn't matter. What I do have firmly in mind is a general sense of that period of our lives, which, since Anna's death, has become familiar to us once again. Beth was thirty-seven. I was thirty-five. There were books on bureaus about "primelife pregnancy," the basal body temperature graph beside the bed, the morning thermometer, our monthly visits to our ob/gyn. Then later, for Beth, there were prescriptions for Clomid, progesterone, a cervical mucous test. And once, for me, a singularly unclimactic semen analysis: me alone in a pure white hospital bathroom, with a Dixie cup in my hand, a plastic pouch in the cup, my manhood on the line, and the whole room in a swirling cold sweat until I fled, careening out the door, my cup empty, fainting flat out on the waiting room floor.

Anna, maybe when you were older, maybe when you were a mother yourself, we might have laughed about this.

Or this: that every time Beth's temperature went up, we seemed to be visiting my parents or hers, their doors open all night, the walls thin. It was like being in high school all over again, on a ratty sofa in a

6

basement den, with your folks "up talking" in the kitchen above. At least once while we were camping with Beth's parents in the Adirondacks, right there in the very midst of what might have become Anna, I remember a cheery camper's call from outside our tent. It was Beth's mom, Betsy, and a whiff of bacon: "Yoo-hoo. Time for breakfast!"

August 26

There are acorns falling from the oak trees these days, hundreds of them, banging down on the tin roof over our back porch. When the wind blows, it sounds like a hailstorm, and if you walk in the yard, you can feel them crunching under your feet. Our next-door neighbor, who has lived in the area all her life, says that the acorns are particularly heavy this year. It means that we will have a "hard winter," she says, and I wonder what exactly she means.

When Anna was born there were no leaves or acorns on the oaks, and I wasn't thinking very much about trees. Some months later, though, I was. Back at the end of March, five weeks after we brought Anna home from the hospital for the first time, some friends of ours gave us a pink dogwood decorated with ribbons, a sapling, no higher than your waist, which we planted in our backyard. We were doing a lot of gardening then. During the warmest parts of the afternoons we'd have Anna out there in the carriage, bundled up, the dog (have I mentioned her name? Jessie, a manic unpurebred retriever) rolling in the sun, and Beth and I up to our elbows in dirt and peat moss, until Anna started fussing. Anyway, the dogwood, in our vocabulary, became "Anna's tree," and I recall having to work around some thick oak roots when I was digging the hole to plant it. I couldn't get the tree exactly where we wanted it, but soon that didn't seem to matter. In May it blossomed, those delicate light pink flowers. It grew thick with leaves, and by mid-June it was as high as my chest.

Then, in a matter of days, it died. The leaves on the lowest branch shriveled. I called the nursery and pruned off the diseased branch, but two mornings later, a Friday, June 16, the leaves on the entire tree had gone pale and wilted. I dug it up, and we all took it

7

back to the nursery, where a salesman cut into the bark with his penknife and said it was already gone, hit by a fungus that "was going around." Beth, who had Anna over her shoulder, told me she thought this meant something, and I told her not to be silly, superstitious. Then the man wrote out a credit slip: $34.95 for "1 dogwood; middle died; Dogwood Blight." Since then we've kept the slip in an old cigar box where we have our unpaid bills and mortgage stubs. Now I have it right here in my hand. And in a few weeks, when their new stock comes in, we will take this slip back to the nursery, get another dogwood, bring it home, and plant it.

August 28

The nursery. How that word rings in my brain. A place to buy dogwoods. A dormer bedroom with a spool crib and impatiens in the window boxes. Or a long room at Georgetown Hospital, fluorescent lit, monitors, alarms, plastic boxes with babies inside, "isolettes," portals for your hands, for your heart, for your whole being to pour through — to touch and hold.

Anna was born with a rare association of physical problems called VATER syndrome. Moments after her birth, one of our doctors told me she had an imperforate anus, her throat ended in a blind pouch, and — this was immediately life threatening — the lower part of her esophagus was connected to her bronchi, already filling her lungs with gastric juices. There would be other tests and other problems that we would learn of later, but this had to be dealt with now.

I remember pushing Anna down the hall from the delivery room to the Intermediate Nursery (Nursery D), still in my blue scrubs, with something like a shower cap on my head. I was so proud and tired, hyped-up and scared. Beth had been through five hours of labor; Anna had flipped back into a breech position. I had eaten three boxes of raisins so I wouldn't faint through the C-section, and now I was literally running between Nursery D where they began prepping Anna for surgery and the maternity wing where Beth was lying, woozy with morphine.

8

"Where is she?" Beth kept asking.

"Around the corner. She'll be all right."

Then I wheeled Beth down to see Anna again. She remembers none of this now; it is all a fog. But I will not forget her holding Anna, really holding her, tight, for the first time. I will not forget holding her myself, and putting her, all warm and wriggling, in one of those portable isolettes with wheels, wires, monitors. Then, with the nurse showing the way, I pushed Anna down to the elevator. We rode to the bottom floor — Surgery — with Anna's silent crying behind the plastic, and a loud beeping sound that was the beat of her heart. She was less than an hour old.

"Do you want a priest? Baptism?" the nurse had asked before we took Anna down. I think I just shook my head. For how, in the circumstances, could I explain that I wasn't Catholic, that I wasn't really anything, that I only truly believed in the necessity of human love and human effort; that I found it hard to believe in a God that might discriminate between a child baptized and a child not? I still find that hard to believe, even harder now. Or to tell you the truth, I find it impossible.

The next time I saw Anna, a few hours later, she was in the Intensive Care Nursery (the ICN) in another isolette that would be her home for nearly the first month of her life. An emergency gastrostomy had been successfully performed to drain her stomach, and another tube had been put through her nose to suction her throat. She was fed with an IV in her hand. Her heart rate, breathing, and oxygen saturation were monitored on digital machines. She was all wires, tubes, and gauze, but she was so beautiful. I was there when she first opened her eyes after the operation. Just as Beth and I were there when she closed them for the very last time. That was precisely two months ago, early in the morning of June 28, when Anna was sedated for her heart surgery. We were in a tiled room on the bottom floor with X rays on the walls and surgical equipment. We were holding Anna in our arms as they shot in the syringe. She was happy, unafraid, and we were there. I say this not so much out of pride, but out of something inside me that fights my own reproach. Something was happening that was wrong and unimaginable. Something was happening that we couldn't stop. Something was happening, but we didn't turn away.

August 29

In the last week, we have been painting the room in the front of our house that is to serve as a study for me and a sort of extension of our tiny living room. It's been a year-long project: first my homemade built-in bookshelves that aren't exactly plumb or square; then the demolition work — myself and a few friends, mostly spindly academics, but on that day like mighty woodsmen, chopping out lath and plaster, opening a doorway, a great swath of light to our living room. Next came the framing, building a header, and hanging the French doors. That was done over the Thanksgiving holiday last year, with the help of Beth's father and younger brother. Beth herself was seven months pregnant with Anna at the time, and in one of our albums we have a photo of her standing sideways between the open two-by-four studs. She is a slender, delicate woman, but with Anna on board, she was all full and globed; she could hardly fit between the studs. Now those studs are covered with wallboard, the joints plastered and sanded. Beth is again slender, almost a swimmer's body, and we have rolled a light gray over the walls and painted the woodwork pure white. Somehow it feels good to be doing this, to draw clean paint over an old surface. It doesn't change anything essential here. It is still hard to look at these floors, these walls, to go into a room without any sound. Yet this is the place where we must live. No one is moving. I can't imagine being anywhere else.

August 30

Just what does it mean for the trees to be gone, with those slivers of light between the leaves? What does it mean to hear a voice, to squeeze a hand, to sense something familiar, then let it go?

August 31

The night before last, Beth dreamed about Anna for the first time. She dreamed that Anna was being cared for in the apartment above ours in the house where we rented a few years ago. Evidently we had worked out a baby-sitting arrangement with the woman who was still living there, and soon we would be driving over to pick Anna up.

So far I have not dreamed at all about Anna, or at least I don't remember my dreaming. In fact, I don't remember any dreams since Anna has died, though I do get up in the middle of the night with things in my head too vivid for dreams. I see a small hospital room all cleared of machines. There are no sounds, no monitors, respirators, or heat lamps. The nurses are gone, the doctors gone. The door is closed behind us. In the window the sun has risen above the trees, traffic is light — it's a holiday morning — and a weary jogger circles a playing field.

Anna lies alone on the freshly made bed. She is different than when we knew her, but once again she is simply herself — no wires, tubes, nothing but her. It is the last time we will hold her. She is swaddled in pink, and her eyes are closed.

September 1

Two days ago, in the afternoon, we went back to the hospital for a meeting with our "genetics counselor." It was odd driving there along the same roads that we traveled so often during Anna's life. There were all the familiar landmarks: the domed cathedral at Catholic University, the winos and drug dealers at Fourteenth and Harvard, the posh shops on Wisconsin Avenue, and the crush of traffic turning into the hospital. During all of Anna's life, the city had been reconstructing a bridge on Michigan Avenue. For a half a year, as we drove back and forth to Georgetown Hospital, we watched this process: the big trucks hauling off rubble, then masons building the stone pillars, the giant girders craned into place, and concrete poured on a mesh of steel. There were detour signs that we always followed, and yesterday,

11

though the signs were gone, the bridge finished, we automatically drove our usual way, squirreling through unlikely side streets.

On our return trip, we still didn't go across that bridge, though at a stoplight, I could see the cars whizzing up over the new smooth surface, heading crosstown, making time. It is an attractive bridge; it speeds traffic; and sometime soon I'm sure I'll drive over it. But not just yet. It doesn't seem right. It's as if this stretch of the road is too simple now, too easy. As if a corner has been cut, or some difficulty skirted by, unacknowledged.

September 2

We are trying to get another baby going — I should say that straightaway. Thus, our meeting with the genetics counselor who has reviewed our family trees and what literature there is on Anna's VATER syndrome. So far, it is unexplained, just as the cause of Anna's death itself is still unexplained, a mystery. These things happen "sporadically" in the population at large. VATER syndrome is unpredictable, undetectable. Something happens, or doesn't happen, about the sixth week of pregnancy. Organs in a line down the middle of a baby's body form abnormally: the heart, trachea, esophagus, ureters, kidneys, and lower GI tract. It is no one's fault. There is no preventing it. It is unlikely to recur in a family, but it is impossible to rule anything out.

So where is the sense in all this? The reason? A child is born with terrible difficulties. She is heroically mended. Loved. She grows, is happy. She dies months later from unknown complications after successful heart surgery, after doctors and nurses have worked for days, around the clock, to save her. Why is there so much devastation in this life? Why take an innocent, joyful child away? I have been told that this could be "all for the best," that she has been "spared much pain," that she is "in the hands of God," or "in a better place."

What extraordinary presumption. Or what blind hope in the face of randomness. Don't tell me there is some beneficent force or being who has everything under control. Don't tell me "he works in mysterious ways." For I cannot understand such ways, and I am not about to give up my own understanding — the only thing I have — for a wisp called faith.

September 4

Labor Day. Another holiday, another anniversary. It is two months since Anna's death. This afternoon we will have hot dogs and barbecued chicken with a group of friends, and that will be good. For it is with friends who knew Anna that we feel most comfortable, people who held her and know what that means, people who have children of their own, or babies they allow — actually want — us to hold.

What I want most is to be reminded of her, and to say what has happened. Without these friends it would all be so much harder — their long listening over cups of coffee, their clear eyes rimming with red. This isn't easy for anyone, but they hear it all and look straight back at us. This, too, I must never forget.

September 5

Anna's first days were a matter of recovering from the surgery (the gastrostomy) performed on the day of her birth. She lived in that plastic isolette in the Intensive Care Nursery. She was cared for around the clock by at least one nurse, often two; and even now, seven months later, I remember their faces and names. Jodie, Angela, Susan, Terri. Their hands in the portals, changing IVs, diapers, electrical leads. Or adjusting her blankets, making her comfortable, and making us all as comfortable as possible.

That night after Anna was born, I slept on a rollaway bed in Beth's room, and the next day, I pushed Beth in a wheelchair down to the ICN, where for a short time the nurses took Anna out of her box and we could hold her, tubes and all, while they watched the monitors. Beth herself had an IV in her arm, and there was a tangle of cords and wires whenever we moved. Mostly Anna slept, but when she

13

awoke, her eyes were wide. She wasn't in pain. On that day her hair seemed to sweep up from both sides, like two giant waves, and crest near the middle. When later, on the phone, a friend asked what she looked like, the only thing I could think of was Elvis, the young Elvis: that waved black hair and big eyes, a little bewildered by all the attention.

September 6

Yesterday afternoon the preliminary autopsy report arrived in the mail. The report is a simple, page-long printout, a list of nine visual observations. There is nothing surprising. It is still unknown exactly what happened to cause Anna's death, but maybe later, when the final histological examination is complete, we will have some better idea.

Until then, we have this, a list of medical observations, as dry as a sales report. They describe various conditions or parts of Anna's body, parts that we knew all along did not work very well.

But this is only the machinery of her, or some of her machinery. There is nothing here about her hair, her pixie smile, or the way, when we took her into a dark room, her eyes would open even wider.

Although I am not a religious man, I think that the spirit of a person continues in the memories of others. I know that Anna fought very hard to live. I know that at some infant level she meant to persevere, to hold tight to those who loved her; I felt that in the squeeze of her hand, and I feel that now.

And while it is true that she died of her ailments — this stark list of medical conditions — it is also true that for a time, she lived in spite of them. She surprised the experts. She was home, a normal kid, for four months. During her last stormy week, twice we were told that Anna was about to die, and twice, as we talked to her and she held our fingers, twice she didn't die. She lived, as though by the force of her own will, something beyond medical explanation, something that in my own mind dwarfs this list of conditions that somehow killed her.

If Anna had survived, someday, when she was a teenager per- haps, I would have taken an odd pleasure in reminding her of what she had come through. I would have told her that if she could come through all that, she could see her way through just about anything.

Then I would have tried to remind myself of the same.

September 7

A friend called last night to say that he and his wife were thinking of us. They have a son who was born about three months after Anna, and I remember Beth and me taking Anna over to Holy Cross Hospital to see their new child sleeping behind a glass window in the nursery. Now our friend says that when he holds his son, he often thinks of Anna and he finds himself crying. I wish that he didn't have to cry, and yet I am terribly grateful for his tears. I want him to cry over this, and to bring my own tears once again to my eyes.

Never before did I understand how important it was, this sharing of grief. It disperses and intensifies it, widens and deepens it. I can't imagine what it would be like without Beth or our friends.

Yet I know that it could be worse. This grief is sharp and deep, but it feels pure and uncomplicated. At five months old, Anna was nothing but innocent. Her needs could be bothersome, tiring, but she was never old enough to do anything that would anger us, that would give us cause for regret.

There is a woman we know in Minnesota whose daughter was hit by a truck and killed in front of their house. Theirs was a normal, healthy, hectic mother-daughter relationship. Yet even now, twenty years later, what this woman remembers most is an argument with her daughter that morning, their harsh words as the girl, Sally, stormed out the kitchen door.

September 8

Because it was clear from the start that Anna wouldn't be nursing for some time (her esophagus ended in a blind pouch), Beth began pumping her breasts and storing her milk in small plastic vials that were stacked in the ICN freezer. The idea was that eventually, if Anna's throat could be repaired, we could feed her mother's milk through a tube, then a bottle, and then, if all went well, she could breast-feed like any other baby. So long before Beth could get out of her hospital bed, she had the electric pump going on the tray-table, that rhythmic whirring sound for fifteen minutes, then I'd label the vials (Loizeaux, Anna, baby girl), date them, and take them, still warm in my hands, down the hall to the freezer.

It would be six days after Anna's birth before Beth left the hospital, and for much of that time, I slept on that rollaway bed. It was a difficult week for both of us, especially for Beth. There is great pain after a Cesarean; there are the usual hormonal changes; and on top of this, our child lay in a plastic box, down a hall, past the nurses' station, and through a set of swinging doors that read "Hospital Personnel," a world away from Beth's arms.

Moreover, it was during these first days that we learned, bit by bit, of the extent and severity of Anna's problems. Each day there were more tests, X rays, ultrasounds, or echocardiagrams. Though she looked perfect on the outside, things were scrambled within. I have already mentioned her imperforate anus and disconnected esophagus. Her kidneys functioned but were oddly shaped (bilateral hydronephrosis), her ureters wide and meandering. Her bladder, vagina, and rectum came together in a common chamber (persistent cloaca). Then lastly, she had an association of heart defects called Tetralogy of Fallot: abnormal openings between her atria and between her ventricles; her aorta emerged from both ventricles instead of one; her right ventricle was enlarged; and there was a narrowing of her pulmonary artery, a condition that, over time, would get worse.

September 11

I mention all this not to appall, but to lay out the medical facts of Anna's life as we learned of them that week. It was frightening. The doctors came to Beth's room and drew us diagrams with explanations and labels. When they shut the door, I would turn to Beth and see in her eyes my own confusion and fear. On the windowsill there were cheery flowers and cards. Kids played soccer on the frosted field across the road. We cried for what seemed to be hours. And then there came a strange feeling — as there still comes to me now — that if I looked at these medical facts hard enough, if I took them all in, learned their names, the language of Anna's frailties, if I watched the echocardia-grams, saw the blood leaking through the holes in her heart, if I stood there and didn't turn my eyes, then I could somehow stare it all down, push it cowering into a corner.

Even during Anna's last hours, I believed at some level that if we kept holding her, kept talking, we could keep her alive.

And perhaps we did, for a very short time. But the final fact is that Anna did die. She is ashes. She is dead now — incredibly — even as I keep on talking.

September 12

Yesterday evening, before dinner, I planted another dogwood in the place in our backyard where Anna's tree had stood. I can see it now through the window where I am working in Beth's study. It is a beautiful tree, about five feet tall. Its leaves are green, lush, and ribbed with veins. When you touch them, they are smooth on the bottom and slightly napped, like felt, on top.

We went back to the nursery last Saturday, and the new trees were in, all lined up in black plastic tubs. There were plenty of pink dogwoods, the kind we originally had, but we decided this time on a different variety, a Chinese dogwood, that is more resistant to fungal diseases. The woman at the cash register accepted our credit slip, and we brought the tree home, crammed in the backseat of the car. On Sunday, it stood regally in the wheelbarrow on our cracked concrete driveway, then yesterday I pushed it across the yard and dug the hole.

It was easy digging, as the earth was still soft and loamy from the last time I had dug there just three months ago. I dug out the same dirt and peat moss that I had shoveled in twice before. I dug up the same shredded pine bark that I had mulched with. And here and there, I even found in the dark dirt the tiny fibrils, like splayed hands: perhaps the most deep and fragile roots of Anna's tree.

Is it smart to be doing this? Or healthy? This planting where something before has died? As I dug deeper my shovel rang against the oak root, thick as your arm, that I had encountered early last spring when daffodils were out and Anna lay bundled up in the carriage. This dogwood, too, I have planted beside that root, in the same ground, with the same hope — though fiercer now, as the last acorns rattle on the roof, and the leaves of the pin oaks turn at the tips.

September 13

About a month after Anna's death, a friend of ours sent us a letter with a poem of May Sarton's enclosed. This morning I read the poem, "An Observation," again.

> *True gardeners cannot bear a glove*
> *Between the sure touch and the tender root,*
> *Must let their hands grow knotted as they move*
> *With a rough sensitivity about*
> *Under the earth, between the rock and shoot,*
> *Never to bruise or wound the hidden fruit.*
> *And so I watched my mother's hands grow scarred,*
> *She who could heal the wounded plant or friend*
> *With the same vulnerable yet rigorous love;*
> *I minded once to see her beauty gnarled,*
> *But now her truth is given me to live,*
> *As I learn for myself we must be hard*
> *To move among the tender with an open hand,*
> *And to stay sensitive up to the end*
> *Pay with some toughness for a gentle world.*

I wish, at some time, I could have read this poem to Anna; or perhaps she would have found it on her own. I wish that I could have meant to her what the mother in this poem meant to the poet. I wish that despite the inevitable arguments, the slamming doors, the walkings out, and reluctant returns — I wish that I could have given Anna a truth to live: "To move among the tender with an open hand," to "Pay with some toughness for a gentle world."

Instead, she has given it to me.

September 14

Over that first week of Anna's life, she got a little better each day, and each day we could take her out of her box a little longer. I suppose that in holding her, we felt very much as any other parents feel in holding a newborn: proud, a little awkward — her strange otherness; already she seemed to have a will of her own, preferring the crook of my left arm to my right, and letting me know it. I remember a profound sense (which I would have for all her life) of her fragility and her toughness, this little six-pound bug with all the hair, who had already been through surgery with only a local anesthetic, and who would be through so much more. As for the wires, tubes, and monitors, it is amazing how quickly we accepted them. We learned what each of them did, and in days they took on an almost comforting familiarity. This small rectangular machine pumped lipids at a prescribed rate into her IV. This vial collected the juices from her stomach, and that one saliva from her throat. An infrared sensor caught her heartbeat. Two leads, attached to her chest, measured her breathing. And there on the screen you could see it graphically: the rolling hills of her breath, and the quick, jagged blips of her heart.

It was reassuring, in fact; and once all these monitors probably saved her. Small newborns, especially premature ones or ones under stress, sometimes have brady spells, times when they simply forget to breathe. One day this happened to Anna. An alarm went off on one of her machines. The nurse — it was Angela — opened the front of the box, shook her, and pumped oxygen into her mouth. Anna breathed again, and the flat line on the screen resumed its rolling geography, those hills that remind me of the Adirondacks, a place we would have

19

liked to take Anna, to show her those rounded mountains, like old men's shoulders.

September 15

About two weeks after Anna died, Beth and I drove up to the Adirondacks, to a place on Piseco Lake where seven years ago we were married. Never before had it been so hard for us to leave home. The previous night we had packed the car with our clothes and camping equipment. We had canceled the newspaper and put timers on the lights. But on that morning, it seemed impossible to go out our front door, to turn the key and walk down the porch stairs with so much left behind. There was a powerful, almost physical, sense of ripping ourselves away. Like some kind of abandonment — the blue box of ashes on top of my bureau, Anna's toys all over, the smell of her still in her unwashed clothing.

I started the car and turned it off. We talked for a while until I could start it again. Then I pulled out of the driveway and onto the road.

A week from today, we will again pack our gear in the car, close the front door, and drive up to the Adirondacks for a weekend visit. I'm sure it will be different this time, though not without pain. In the mountains, the maples should be turning red and orange. The grasses and alders in the vleis will be tan and brown and crackle in the wind. At night there could be frost, and lying in our tent, in the place where Anna was conceived, we will pull our sleeping bags over our shoulders.

September 18

I think it was on Monday or Tuesday, January 23 or 24, that I came home for the night for the first time since Anna's birth. Beth was gaining strength and Anna was stable. I remember coming in the door and greeting Jessie, who had been tended by our friends for the past few days. There was a pile of mail on the dining room table, and dog hair, like tumbleweed, on the floor. Upstairs in the bathroom, towels lay about, still heavy and wet with amniotic fluid. Beth's side of the bed was still soaked, and it struck me that this couldn't have happened just a few nights before: Beth sitting up rigid in bed, then running for the bathroom; and me trying to be cool, calm, calling the doctor, shaking like a leaf, forgetting my wallet, keys, remembering to turn down the thermostat.

I collected the wet linen, took it downstairs, and started a wash. It was almost midnight, but I was wildly exhausted. I vacuumed the house and scoured the sinks and tubs. Then I went out for a jog around our neighborhood, my usual route, past the rows of squat bungalows on our street, the porch swings still, the dogs curled and quiet behind chain link fences. I ran up around the old Masonic Lodge and the Independent Order of Oddfellows. Coming down our own street again, I passed our house, taking it in as a stranger might see it: another sleepy bungalow with scraggly yews as high as the porch railing, a concrete walk, milky in the moonlight, a three-window dormer behind a bare pin oak overhanging the street.

How many times have I jogged by our house and seen in its clean, spare lines no hint of trouble? In the spring and summer, we have white flower boxes on the railings and below each dormer window. When Anna was home, I would see in those three windows the glow of her night-light beyond the flowers, and often I would see the top of Beth's head, slowly moving, and I would know she was rocking in the chair beside the crib, nursing Anna.

But on that night, as on these mild September nights, there was no light in the window, and I remember trying to imagine what it would be like if this child were to die.

What is surprising, and perhaps frightening, is that I *could* almost imagine it. I could almost feel its sheer weight and exhaustion. The aimless anger. I even saw Beth and myself going away to a clear, clean place. I saw myself at home doing small, achievable jobs.

Could I have known then that I was steeling myself for this? Could I, in just imagining, have somehow brought all this about?

No, I don't believe that, though sometimes I wonder.

21

September 19

What I couldn't imagine that night as I ran past our house was what Anna's death might be like for her. In the end, my imagination then and now is terribly limited or selfish, a kind of envisioning of my own survival, not an imagining of her death itself. To do so, I suppose, would be awfully close to imagining my own death — not just that vague sense that, as certain as taxes, we will all die, but I mean the real dying part of it, the time when you know that yes, this is it, and it is there right in front of you.

What did Anna sense of this? And what will my own sense of it be? Was it like a spiraling down? Or a fading away? Or a rising, like mist on a glassy lake? Or was it more sudden, fierce, the pull of a waterfall, a tearing away, that last beat of her heart — not a giving in, but a clench?

There are times when I am involved with something else that I almost forget Anna. There are other times when I want to remember her, but she seems so far away. And then there are times, unexpected and unprepared for, when she comes to me so vividly that she is almost there.

Yesterday evening I was arranging my desk in my study, which we have finished painting and I will soon move into. I was putting some old letters in a drawer, when I thought I could feel Anna over my shoulder, her arms hanging loose, relaxed, that damp, drooly spot near my collarbone. I have held a good number of kids, and they all feel different. Anna was long and light and limber. Except for when she was crying, she would mold to your shoulder and chest. I had a way of carrying her with one arm, my left. It made me feel cocky, a father. She would have her head on my shoulder, and I would have my forearm beneath her rump and my hand around her right leg, just above her ankle. I remember the narrow fold of flesh that was there, and the curl and splay of her toes. I could even show you exactly the size of her leg where I held it, if you could just see the circle I make when I touch my thumb and index finger.

Someday, I have read, the sudden presence of a lost and loved one will be consoling. And yes, I want these moments to happen, this strange sense of her proximity, the smell of her skin in the air. But this is not consoling. There is no peace in this. When I feel her presence, I feel her loss. I feel it right here in my hands.

September 20

Before I continue, there is something else I should say that touches on the limits of my own imagination. It is the question of what Beth has been through, her suffering, much of which I share, though some of which I can only try to imagine.

Beth is a woman of quiet strength, warmth, and intellect. She is an English professor, though she has always said that what she most wanted in life was to be a mother. Three years ago she had a miscarriage, and after that, getting pregnant was difficult. But when Anna arrived, even with all her problems, we thought we were the luckiest parents in the world.

As I think of Beth and Anna together, what I see is a kind of wholeness or completion, yet something very different from the dewy images we find in television or magazine advertisements for baby products. Beth is nearly forty years old. Her face is soft and round, her eyes large, dark, and shallow-set, the eyes from which Anna's were born. She keeps her thick black hair at medium length, pulled neatly back at the sides and parted in front where there has been, since I've known her, a wide undisguised swatch of gray. Long ago she took ballet lessons and performed while she was in high school. She is still interested in dance, and though she hasn't practiced in years, there remains in the way that she carries herself — even in the most domestic of tasks — a certain calm, a control and economy of movement. I saw this calm particularly as she walked across a room with Anna in her long narrow arms. She'd move slowly, quietly, pausing and rocking on the balls of her feet, her face strangely still, smoothed, as though seen in twilight. She'd have Anna snug to her chest, with her lips in Anna's hair. To look at them, you would see them as one, moving as one — the same eyes, same hair, and Anna all nestled in and enfolded.

Yet I wouldn't call it joy, what I saw in Beth then. She was often tired, her eyelids heavy, with dark circles below. There could even be a tinge of sorrow there, as though she knew that Anna might be our last. But what I mostly remember when I think of them together — walking across a room, or sitting in the rocking chair, nursing — what I will always remember was a deep serenity, deeper than words, deeper than thought. It had to do with the absolute rightness of the two of them like that, despite the problems. There was that depth in the eyes of an older mother whose child has been hard to come by.

What could it mean to sever *that* link? It is staggering to think of. Beth's love for and patience with Anna were unbounded. In late February, when Anna had to return to the hospital for a week with a urinary tract infection, Beth stayed in her room every night to nurse her, while I went home and slept in our bed. Months later, during Anna's heart surgery and for days immediately thereafter, Beth pumped her breasts to keep up her supply for when Anna could nurse again. But then, when Anna died, Beth had to literally wean herself of Anna. Slowly she had to produce less and less milk for a child who wasn't there. I remember sitting on our bed about noon on the Fourth of July. We had just gotten home from the hospital, and Beth had to pump to relieve the pressure. Outside it was raining lightly. The bassinet was empty in the corner of our room. I turned on the switch, and there was the familiar rhythmic throb of the pump on the bedside table. We waited a moment. Beth's milk came out, but it had turned thin and green.

Her body knew. Every part of her knew. There is this aspect of her knowledge — her bodily knowledge — that, as a man, I simply can't share. And yet to think of it and imagine it still takes my breath away.

September 21

There is an uncontrollable shudder and a low, inside, animal sound that comes at the depth of grief, or perhaps it's at the height of fear. I had never felt this, or heard this sound from my own body before. It was surprising and alien, from so far inside that it couldn't have been me, though of course it was. It came to me twice: once, in the hospital when I truly knew that Anna would die; and then as we sat on the edge of our bed, when Beth's milk turned green.

What are the limits of human suffering and sadness? It is so appalling, because I know there is much worse. I think of widows or widowers without anyone left to share their grief. I think of survivors of the Holocaust who saw their families slaughtered before their eyes. I know that my own sorrow, so large to me, is nothing compared to the suffering of others.

And still, I must speak it. There is nothing else to do. When Beth had finished pumping, I took the vials of milk down the hall, that old warmth in my hands. In the bathroom I ran water and poured the greenish liquid down the drain.

Soon after I finish writing this entry, I will pack the car, and this evening we will head up to the Adirondacks, stopping overnight at my parents' house in New Jersey. I am aware that on this day, if Anna had lived, she would have been eight months old; and Beth and I will probably talk about this as we plow up Route 95. It is sad to think of, though at the moment I can actually smile when I look at her photos. I bet her hair would have been even longer by now, even more unruly. I bet she would have grown a little faster with her mended heart. She might even have been crawling, or eating a little cereal or that stuff that Gerber's puts into jars. If Anna were on this trip, I'm sure that Beth would be sitting in the backseat on one side of her, and Jessie on the other. I'm sure at some point that Anna would be crying, spitting up, the dog licking her hands. I'm sure it would be hectic, wild. "Slow down!" "Pull over. She's puked everywhere! . . ."

Just as I'm sure that tonight as I drive with the traffic thinning and Beth dozing in the seat beside me — I am sure that at some moment I will feel suddenly lost on this familiar road, with its familiar signs and rest areas, the whir of the motor, and nothing but headlights in the rearview mirror.

September 26

We are back from the Adirondacks, where, as luck would have it, the remains of Hurricane Hugo (winds of forty to fifty miles per hour) arrived a few hours after we had pitched our tent on the beach at Piseco Lake. It was a wild, sleepless night, one I would go through again, though I wouldn't make a habit of it.

On the car radio, we had heard all the weather reports as we traveled north. Charleston had been devastated the day before. The storm, diminishing in intensity, had passed through West Virginia, Pennsylvania, and the tracking predictions had it curling east through New England, though of course no one could be sure. In any case, the Adirondacks would be windy and rainy that night. Streams might swell. People were advised to have flashlights ready. There could be power outages.

How different you are when you have a child, and when you don't. If Anna was with us, we would never have pitched our tent beside the lake that night — we wouldn't have even thought about it. We would have stayed in the lodge a few hundred yards away from the beach, and we would have heard, from our warm beds, the wind rattling the shutters and rain on the windowpanes. We might have even heard a tree go down, or brittle shingles ripping from the roof. But we wouldn't actually have been *out in it*, or as far out in it as a tent allows.

There may be a kind of recklessness, or daring, or foolishness, that comes with grief, as if after one terrible mishap, something inside of you simply lets go. You don't care so much about your appearance, your health, job, or your usual diversions. You play tennis and hit ten straight balls into the net, throwing the match, just to see how it feels. Or you pitch your tent not far from a large tree, knowing full well that a storm is coming, that the body is frail, the wind erratic, that tall trees do fall, and nothing could ever be predictable or "unlikely" again.

So we spent that night in the storm, the weight of our bodies holding the tent to the ground. Rain, atomized, shot through the nylon fabric. Our bed rolls were soaked. The wind filled the tent, ballooning it. It shuddered and yawed, but it did not tear.

Then, by five in the morning, the storm had passed. The tree had not fallen. No lightning had struck. With the first light, the lake was smooth and quiet; the mist had already gone. It was up in the hills, ragged bits of it, hanging like smoke in the trees.

September 27

On the morning after my first night at home after Anna's birth, I returned to the hospital to find Beth's room crowded with nurses. She had just fainted in the shower, her black hair still wet and sudsy, her face pale, tears in her eyes. The nurses had helped her back into bed, and eventually they left the room. She drank some juice and I sat beside her. Shaking her head, she said that all she wanted was to be clean for the first time since Anna's birth. She wanted to wash her hair and comb it, so she could look good when we'd visit Anna that morning.

After a while she felt strong enough to put her legs back over the side of the bed. I remember helping her up, her grasp trembling but firm as she moved slowly toward the sink. It was as if nothing was more important than getting there and doing what had to be done. She let go of my arm and bowed her head beneath the warm-running spigot. She rinsed her hair, then patted it with a towel. When she combed it out, it was shining and clean, as beautiful as I've ever seen it. Then, by herself, she moved back to the edge of the bed and sat there carefully to let it dry.

Beth had fainted because she was still weak from the Cesarean, the nurses had said, though of course it was much more than that. It was everything in our world that had buckled her legs and then had made her walk, so determined, to the sink. While I had been out running the night before, she, too, must have imagined what it would be like if Anna were to die. Perhaps she had thought of holding her, so still and cold in her arms. Or perhaps she had thought of laying her down on a freshly made bed and never holding her again.

If I had to do it all over, I never would have left the hospital that night before. From then until the day Beth came home, I slept on the rollaway bed.

In the mornings we'd get up and eat hospital food on plastic trays. I'd push Beth down the hall in a wheelchair, and through the double doors. At the sink outside the ICN, we'd wash our hands and arms with a small scrub brush and antiseptic soap. Then we'd put on our sanitary aprons and go in. Anna's isolette was always up on the right-hand side next to the window that looked out across Reservoir Road and through some bare trees toward that soccer field. You couldn't see Anna from the doorway — just the blue end of her isolette — but I remember with what anticipation we would go in there and move toward her. Was she awake? Sleeping? What had happened during the night? Any brady spells? Any signs of infection? What was her urine output? Bilirubin count? Was she still getting better? Was she still just the cutest thing in the world?

I don't care how old I get, or how world-weary or cynical, I hope I never forget what it was like to get up in the morning and see my daughter, even as she lay in a plastic box with all those tubes, catheters, and wires. There was so much life in there, so much in all of us.

September 28

We'd stay in the ICN for most of the morning, or until Beth got tired and had to go back to her room. We'd hold Anna for perhaps a half hour at a time. She would be bundled up in layers of receiving blankets, and except for the gastrostomy tube into her stomach and the tube into her right nostril, fixed there with a piece of adhesive tape, she looked perfectly healthy, even happy.

When she was born, her hands were in fists, and slowly during those early days in the ICN, they began to unfold, her fingers long and tapered. I recall the first time when I could lay my own finger across her palm, and she would close hers around it. I also recall the first time I put my pinky in her mouth. It was against doctor's orders — she wasn't supposed to have a pacifier of any kind — but right then she was crying, and the nurses, checking the hallway for any sign of our pediatric surgeon, said go ahead, give it a try, it won't hurt her.

How can you not be amazed at the power of a child's suck, and the power of giving comfort? It was as if all of Anna's strength was centered there in her mouth; and it was a long time before I pulled out my finger, all red and pruned, and she fast asleep, her lips faintly quivering. What a feeling that was.

September 29

While Beth was recovering, I spent a lot of time shuttling between the ICN and Beth's room, taking vials of milk to the freezer, checking in on Anna, talking with the neonatologists, then heading back up the hall with whatever information I could pass along to Beth. When I think back on it, my overall impression is one of tiredness, and yet a sort of wild exuberance when there was something I could do. The nurses must have sensed this, and they began giving me little jobs: to change and weigh Anna's diaper, or to clean up the mucousy discharge around the tube where it went into her nose.

I know that none of this seems very sumptuous now, but at the time these little things seemed filled with strange wonder and importance. If Anna's diaper was sodden, it meant that her kidneys, though deformed, were still working. And if her kidneys were working, and if her heart kept working, and if they could repair her esophagus, and ward off infections in her urinary and GI tracts — if all this happened, then she would live.

In the end, it *was* Anna's kidneys that finally failed. For some unknown reason after her heart surgery, her kidneys simply shut down. She couldn't urinate. She took on fluid, and this beautiful, delicate child more than doubled her weight, utterly transforming her, in just a few days before she died.

I tell you, there is nothing so wondrous as a diaper, warm and weighty with urine. Open your hamper and breathe it all in. Stick your hand in there and squeeze. I would do anything to feel that again.

October 2

I made a point of being in the ICN each afternoon between four and five when the doctors did their rounds. Perhaps because George-town is a teaching hospital, they didn't mind people looking over their shoulders and asking questions. Basically the word was, so far so good. Anna was gaining strength each day. Her heart kept pumping. The heavy doses of IV antibiotics had kept her free of infection, though their effectiveness would diminish over time. If Anna continued to improve, then early the next week, Dr. Hoy, the pediatric surgeon who had performed the gastrostomy, would attempt to repair her esophagus and tie off the fistula (or passageway) that connected the lower part of her esophagus with her bronchi. He would also insert directly into her heart a Broviac catheter (or a wider IV tube) through which they could better feed her while she recovered. Finally, he would perform a colostomy, diverting the contents of her colon out-side her body and into a bag, so they wouldn't mix with (and infect) her urine in that common bladder-vaginal-rectal chamber.

Taken individually, each of these procedures was rather straight-forward, yet not without risks or problems. Colostomies are performed very frequently, even on children this size. Broviac catheters are almost as common, though they involve a "small" (5 percent) risk of infection, which could lead to further complications, even death.

The repair of Anna's esophagus, though, presented more trouble. In almost all humans, the aorta, the largest vessel in the body, swings around the left-hand side of the heart; and surgeons, when they operate on the esophagus, go in from the right-hand side of the chest. In a murky sonogram, however, it seemed that Anna's aorta looped around on the wrong (the right-hand) side of her heart. This meant that Dr. Hoy would have to go in from the left, an unusual route, and even if he could get to her esophagus, there was no certainty that he could mend it. If the two detached ends of her

30

esophagus were not far apart, they could be stretched and sewn together. But if they were too distant, then a later operation, involving tissue transplantation, would be the only solution. In that case, the best he could do for the time being would be to insert a "spit fistula," or a tube that would drain the upper part of her throat, like a spigot coming out of the side of her neck.

As if all of this was not complicating enough, there was then the overwhelming question of Anna's heart. She had Tetralogy of Fallot. Her heart was deformed; it didn't work efficiently. But was it strong enough to pump her through seven hours of anesthesia, surgery, and what would surely be a rocky recovery? The truth was that no one really knew. The cardiologists said "she had a pretty good shot," though we had come to a place where machines and knowledge could only tell us so much. The rest was something like intuition, a hunch, hope, and the peculiar power of a person to live.

I recall when I asked Dr. Hoy to come down to Beth's room after he had learned of the extent of Anna's heart condition. He was a blocky man, serious, with squarish glasses and a kind smile. His voice was low and somber. He closed the door behind him, leaving his resident out in the hall. He said this wouldn't be easy, but the odds were with us. He said there was really no alternative, that this was the time; and we told him we'd like him to go ahead and try.

October 3

In the meantime, Beth's parents, Carl and Betsy, had arrived on January 25 with take-out Chinese food, which we ate in Beth's room. On the 27th, my sister Chris, herself six months pregnant, flew up from North Carolina to spend a few hours with us. Each day I talked with my parents on the phone, and each night, about dinnertime, I called a few of our friends. These calls were like a lifeline for me, especially when Beth was still foggy with pain and drugs. There is no world so enclosed as a hospital, especially an Intensive Care Nursery. There is no real night or day, hours ooze one into another; the monitors flash and beep. I can't tell you how good it felt to hear a

31

warm voice on the other end of the line, or to hear the clatter of dishes, silverware: tables being set in dining rooms where we had sat and would sit again.

On January 28, a week after Anna's birth, Beth was discharged from the hospital. She was wearing a white turtleneck beneath a pink cable-knit sweater. She had on small gold hoop earrings, running shoes, and baggy sweatpants. She sat in the corner chair as I made four trips, back and forth to the car, carrying down our clothes, kit bags, flowers, cards, a radio, and that framed photo of Piseco Lake that Beth kept on her bedside table. The room seemed odd when I had cleared it out, and it seemed stranger still to think of someone else coming in there, a brand-new mother, another proud, awkward father, and a different gallery of flowers and cards on the windowsill. For a week we had lived there, just as five months later we would live for another week in another room in another part of the hospital during Anna's last days. At neither of those times did we want to leave — there was so much uncompleted. But the nurse was coming now with the wheelchair. We had signed the papers. We had spent our time with Anna, and we would see her again tomorrow.

So Beth stepped gently into the wheelchair, and the nurse led us down the hall and down the elevator. She took us to the Emergency Room door where outside the night air was cold and blustery, our breath coming out in white plumes. I pulled up the car and Beth got in slowly, but without needing help. As we waited at the traffic light on Reservoir Road, we could see the fluorescent lights in the fifth-floor windows. They were the brightest windows in the whole hospital; and as I see them now — that long row of them — I count one, two, three from the left-hand end: a window like any other, closed but unblinded. It's pouring blue light out into the wind.

October 4

Anna has been dead now for three months, and still we have not put away her things or even cleaned up those little splatters of spit-up on the floor. Her wind-up swing stands stiltlike in front of the hearth;

her playpen, crammed with toys, is right there in the corner. I can see them from where I am sitting.

About a week ago, I moved in here, my new study in the front of the house. There are books on the shelves. The walls are light gray, the trim fresh and white, and there is the faint scent of the linseed oil and turpentine that we used to clean and polish this old desk that was once my father's. Through the French doors you can walk into our living room. Or you can look through the front windows and over the porch railing and flower boxes, to the sidewalk and the pin oak that is beginning to lose its leaves.

I am happy to be here. This is the first time I have had a study of my own. But I will miss that small room on the back of our house. It was where I worked while Anna was alive.

October 5

Back then I was struggling to write a novella, and often, when it was my turn with Anna, I would try to get some writing done at the same time that I was taking care of her. In that back room there was just enough space for myself, the desk, a portable radiator, and the Swyngomatic. I'd get her settled in the seat and pile the tray with toys. Then I'd wind up the machine, let it rip, and until Anna was about four and a half months old, she'd swing there for two or three hours at a stretch, either sleeping, fooling with her toys, or just looking around while I beat on the typewriter. Every fifteen minutes I'd wind the machine, a sound like a million crickets. Then there'd be that rhythmic click-clunk, click-clunk, her hair flying, bubbles in her mouth, until the machine wound down and I'd quick have to wind it up again before she'd start making a fuss.

At first I felt slightly guilty about this. What was the effect of all this swinging, her world arcing back and forth? But she seemed happy. I was happy. I'd read her the stuff I was writing, and sometimes I swear I saw in her eyes the faintest hint of profound interest. She was enthralled!

By the time she was five months old, though, the honeymoon

with the Swyngomatic was over. She got too wise. She knew when she was being diverted, and she knew when my attention was focused on something other than her. I tried everything. New toys, rattles. I read my stuff even more dramatically. But no, not a chance.

In the end she just wanted to be held, and not without some mild resentment, I'd push back the typewriter and take her, crying, out of her swing. If the weather was good, we'd go out in the backyard beneath the oaks where there is another kind of swing: an old home-made bench-swing constructed of painted oak floorboards suspended from a frame of welded radiator pipes. I'd sit there and we'd go back and forth, the whole frame swaying. I'd have Anna in my left arm, and she'd be looking up, maybe not at me, but at something higher up than me. Her eyes would be huge, delighted. Her fussiness would momentarily stop. She would be smiling, and then I'd follow her gaze. I'd look up to where she was looking and see the undersides of the oak trees, the light shimmering through the chinks in the leaves.

That is what Anna meant to me. Without her being there, I never would have been slightly annoyed. I never would have felt her need and taken myself away from myself. I never would have gone outside with the weight of another life in the crook of my arm. I never, on my own, would have looked up and seen.

October 9

Last night we returned from a weekend trip to North Carolina to be on hand for the baptism of my niece, Lisa Jane, the daughter of my sister Chris. Lisa is six months old now. She was born about three months after Anna, and she is doing a lot of those baby things that Anna was doing in the weeks before she died: that groping and grasping for objects placed in front of her, and then the inevitable pushing of everything into her mouth. When I hold Lisa I am struck anew by the wonder of this life, that the lungs breathe, capillaries dilate, the heart pumps, muscles contract, and a small hand opens and closes. Yet at the same time, I am also struck by a wave of coldness, a hard, sharp, metallic thing. What I feel is so much difference, or distance. This wonderful thing is not my child. This is not the same. And now it makes me wonder if I will ever wholly open my arms again — even, if possible, for another child of my own.

On our way down there, and then again on our way back, we passed over the North and South Anna rivers. They originate near Lake Anna, about thirty-five miles northwest of Richmond. They flow under Route 95 and come together just east of the highway near a place called Kings Dominion, a giant amusement park for children. From there the Anna River meanders southeast through sparsely populated Virginia countryside, and at a place undesignated on my map, it becomes the Pamunkey River, which in turn flows into the York, which empties into the Chesapeake, which finally becomes the Atlantic Ocean.

I don't know if we would ever have taken Anna to Kings Dominion, but I am sure that we would have gone with her sometime to the ocean. There would have been plastic buckets and plastic shovels. There would have been sunburn, and sand in diapers. We would have put one of those big floppy hats on her head, and someday, when she was strong enough, we might have carried her, scared and excited, out into the waves.

October 10

Do we still cry about this, some three months later? The answer is yes. Of course.

The sadness comes in waves, perhaps with less frequency than early on, but still with the same intensity. It is hard to predict, though it seems to come often on weekends, when we are trying to relax or catch up on chores around the house. I'll be vacuuming the carpet up in Anna's room where the dog likes to lie. Or I'll take out the trash and be struck by the new crispness in the air. It has been getting cooler these days, in the forties at night. The leaves are still green on Anna's new tree and on the tall oaks in the backyard. But the light is different. A season has passed. Acorns cover the yard, and soon I will be bringing in the potted plants and carrying the storm doors up from the cellar.

A year ago I was building these bookshelves, Beth wore baggy sweaters, and we had just gotten the results from the amniocentesis. The baby seemed fine. The chromosomes were normal. Our doctor could tell us the child's sex, but we decided to live with the mystery, to give space to our imaginings, to be utterly surprised.

Now there is once again that crisp anticipation in the air. It is fall. When I go out jogging I wear a sweatshirt; I see my breath; and sometimes, as I run, I catch myself thinking that if I could only figure it out, if I could understand this thing, sort it through, then somehow I could get Anna back. I could find her and bring her home.

Tonight when I returned to the house, it was warm inside and there were crickets ratcheting behind the stove. I took off my sweatshirt. I heard an odd sound in the basement. And when I went down there, Beth was bent over the washing machine, covering her face and crying into a shirt of Anna's that is still stained with spots of her pink medicine — though it doesn't smell like her anymore.

October 11

We cry a lot together, and a lot on our own. On the shelf to the right of my desk I have four pictures of Anna hanging on pins that I've stuck into the bindings of books there. In one of them, my favorite, she is sitting in her swing, and she is delighted by something, giggling, her eyes so wide and faintly mischievous, her hands together brought up close to her chin. Her right foot sticks out from the blanket in which she is wrapped. Her tongue is on the edge of her lips, and her hair is simply ridiculous: long swatches of it, like duck tails, hanging on either side of her face. She is all disheveled and happy — windblown, an elf — the way that I most remember her.

On the other side of my desk now I am looking at a photocopy of Anna's chromosomes, made after the amniocentesis. It is photo #8-10 from lab #88-0574, dated 9/16/88. The chromosomes are twenty-three matched pairs, the last a double X. They are strange squiggly things, elongated, segmented, like worms turning this way and that. It is hard to believe that inside of them was a kind of blueprint for the little person smiling to my right in the swing. It is hard to believe that these chromosomes are utterly unique. And it is so hard to believe — though I do understand — that there will never again be anything exactly like this in the world.

October 12

At about 9:00 A.M. on Tuesday, January 31, the surgery to repair Anna's esophagus began. Since the previous Saturday when Beth was discharged, we had come into the hospital for most of each day, and at night, before we went to bed, we called the ICN and talked to Anna's nurse, then called again in the morning when we got up. On that Tuesday we drove in early, with the headlights on and the defroster whirring. Anna was in her isolette beside the window as always, and we were able to take her out and hold her for about an hour before they had to get her ready to go downstairs.

That morning we took a lot of photographs, which we now have in an album. In them we look like any other parents holding a child all bundled in blankets. Beth is wearing that same white turtleneck and pink cabled sweater. In many of the photos she is talking to Anna, or singing, and in one Anna is looking directly at her, a little quizzical, nonplussed, and she is holding Beth's index finger in her hand.

The nurse in charge of Anna that morning was Angela Smith, an African-American woman, about twenty-five, with small freckles across her cheekbones, and her hair pulled back in a thick braid. Angela had taken shifts with Anna a number of times before; and I know I am right in saying that her care was more than what was professionally required. My sister Meg was once a pediatric nurse, and she has told me how attached she often became to certain children on her floor. Even now, more than a decade later, she still remembers their names, faces, the diseases they had, and whether they lived or died.

I think that something like this may have happened between

Angela and Anna; and I think something like this also happened between myself, Beth, and Angela. There is little so moving to a parent as to see another person, someone you hardly know, holding your sick child, ministering to her, as if that child were her own.

Angela did that. And while our lives have already diverged, I hope I will never forget her brown hand on Anna's hair. Or what she told me months later, when I called to tell her that Anna had died. She said that she had always enjoyed taking care of Anna. She said that we had a beautiful child, that we were good parents, and that she would never forget Anna's eyes.

October 13

So on that Tuesday morning, when we heard that Angela would be with Anna throughout her surgery, it came as a kind of comfort, even as she took Anna from our arms and lay her in the portable isolette to go downstairs. She reconnected various wires, IV lines, and there was again that beeping sound, like a truck backing up, that was the sound of Anna's heart. Next came the phone call from Dr. Hoy in the operating room to say that everything was ready. Beth was walking by now, but deliberately; and very deliberately, with Angela alongside, we pushed Anna out of the ICN, through the double doors, and down the hall to the elevator. At the bottom floor — Surgery — Beth and I weren't allowed to go any farther, so we bent over the isolette once more. Anna was awake; I remember that. But what frightens me now is that somehow I have already forgotten precisely what she looked like then, whether she was crying, or complacent, or wide-eyed and bewildered. It could have been the last time that we would see her alive, and I must have tried to fix the image in mind. But for the life of me, it still doesn't come.

What does come, however, is that thinning rectangle of light as the elevator door pulled closed. The last thing I saw was the sloped glass sides of the isolette, like a tiny greenhouse in the sun. Angela was in her pale blue scrubs with matching elastic booties over her shoes. She had her hands on the long bar on the end of the isolette in the way that you'd push a shopping cart. She was looking back at us, making a smile, waiting until the door closed before she'd take Anna away.

October 16

During the surgery we stayed in a waiting room on the maternity wing, just a few doors away from Beth's old room. There was a TV, bathroom, Scandinavian wood chairs with maroon cushions, and drapes, in matching maroon, that smelled of old cigarettes. I was trying to read Peter Taylor's *The Old Forest* for a class I would teach the next week, and Beth was knitting something, probably for Anna, though I'm not sure what.

The previous day we had arranged for Dr. Hoy's resident to periodically come up from surgery and tell us how things were going. At about 10:30 she knocked for the first time on the door. She said that Anna was under sedation, that the Broviac catheter into her heart had been successfully implanted, and she was doing well. Two hours later she returned again, sooner than we had expected, with the news that the murky sonogram had been misinterpreted. Dr. Hoy had gone in on Anna's left side as planned, but he had found her aorta there, exactly where it should have been. Now, after sewing up that incision, he had gone in from the right side, the usual procedure, and it appeared that indeed, if Anna could sustain herself through the operation, her esophagus *could* be mended. The detached ends were not too far apart.

October 17

The rest of that afternoon — or until Anna returned from surgery — is blurry to me now, though I'm sure we must have had lunch in the cafeteria and perhaps we walked outside to breathe some fresh air. I doubt I got very much reading done, though the book was often in my hand. Still, I can't think of *The Old Forest* without thinking of that maroon room and our wait for Anna. In the title story an old man recalls an adventure of his youth, when he and a girlfriend were involved in an car accident after which the girl inexplicably ran away, disappeared, and he had to search and search for her.

At any rate, it wasn't until 3:30 that the resident knocked again on the door. She said that Anna's esophagus had been repaired and the fistula to her bronchi had been tied off. The colostomy was being performed now; her heart had kept right on pumping. It would be an hour or so before they'd bring her back up again.

So at 4:30 we went through the double doors and waited outside the ICN. Soon there was a call from downstairs to make sure that everything was ready. And then, a little before 5:00 P.M., I remember them coming around the corner and through the double doors, pushing the isolette in front of them. There were at least a dozen people: nurses, technicians, a cardiologist, anesthesiologists, all in their pale blue scrubs, booties, and shower caps. They were hustling, sweating, and talking, a crowd surging down a tunnel. They couldn't pause when they came by us — they had to get Anna inside. But I recall Angela smiling with exhaustion, relief, and a hint of caution. She'd talk to us later.

Through the glass top of the isolette we caught a glimpse of Anna. She was splayed out, naked and ashen. There were new dressings and tubes. Her eyes were closed; she wasn't moving; but the hall rang with the beat of her heart.

It took about forty-five minutes for them to get Anna settled in the ICN, and through the doorway we watched them bustling around her, hooking up tubes, wires, and machines. While we waited, Dr. Hoy came through the swinging doors. He was out of his surgical gear, in a coat and tie. He had a Coke in his hand, and he was tired, sweating. He said that everything had gone as well as it could have, though it would be a few days before Anna would be out of the woods. I asked him if he had had any lunch, and he said no, that all the time he and his team had been in the operating room, kept at ninety degrees Fahrenheit so that Anna's body temperature wouldn't fall. "It was like a sauna," he said.

I remember thanking him profusely and awkwardly, and his replying that we had Anna mostly to thank — she was stronger than they had expected. Then I asked him how he knew that, and he switched his Coke to his left hand so he could hold out his right and carefully close his fingers, as if around something small and fragile, like a plum.

"I held her heart in my hand," he said, with nothing but wonder and reverence for the thing in his fingers. "I felt it beating." It was as though he himself could hardly believe it.

October 18

When at last we went back in the ICN, Anna was not in an isolette, but on a small elevated crib, like a tray, beneath an automatic heat lamp. She lay on her back, naked, except for patches of tape and gauze. Her hair was matted, her arms out limp to the sides, her legs crossed in that position in which she was born. Her head was turned to her left where the tube from the respirator was taped in her mouth. Her chest went up and down with eerie regularity, that rhythmic, chuffing breath of the machine. The Broviac catheter, a quarter-inch tube, emerged from a wide dressing on the right-hand side of her chest. Two other half-inch tubes, one one each side, drained blood and fluid from her chest cavity. There were the familiar red and green leads on her leg and under her arms, leads to the heart and breathing monitors, a whole bank of them now, on the counter beside the window. In surgery, Dr. Hoy had replaced the gastrostomy dressing and rubber tube that came out of her stomach. A gauze pad lay on the left side of her abdomen, the site of her colostomy. Beneath it were the two ends of her colon (two stoma) where it had been severed, each brought to the surface of her skin, about an inch apart. One was active, the other not. When you looked at them, they were like two small roses, pink and puckered, the size of dimes.

October 19

Why do I tell you all this? Why describe every wire and tube? Or the grainy, foul, mustard-colored liquid that came out of her colon and soaked into the gauze pad?

Because there was no looking around it then, and there is no looking around it now. Because we are all wires and tubes covered over with skin. Because I still smell that soaked gauze pad, and practically keel over thinking of it. Because I hear the respirator and see the dials and flashing digital readouts. Because I still yearn for that tangle of love and machinery, the focus of it, the way it all worked so that Anna might live.

October 21

We stayed late at the hospital that night. Angela worked overtime. Every half hour she took blood samples from Anna and sent them across to the lab. She told us about the surgery, about the heat and tension as Dr. Hoy appoached Anna's esophagus from the left-hand side, and then the relief when he had finished the procedure. She explained all the new wires and tubes and the results of the blood tests. There was a problem with Anna's blood CO_2 level, and the doctors would be watching that closely. Finally Angela had to leave — her next shift was 7:00 A.M. She briefed the nurse who was replacing her and checked the monitors. For a long moment she looked at Anna very carefully, almost privately, perhaps in the way that she watched over her during all that surgery. Then she turned quickly and went out the door. The last thing she said — to us, not herself — was "Get some sleep."

Laid out on the crib, Anna looked so small and vulnerable. Her skin was pale, her body still, except for that rise and fall of her chest. There was an extraordinary urge to just put a blanket over her, or to take her into our arms, though of course we couldn't do that. All we could do was to hold her hand and stroke her skin and hair. Months later she would be laid out again like that, and again we would crane over the crib and touch her with our hands.

What kind of things are these fingers and thumbs? How much can pass through and beyond them? Or how much just rams against an elastic wall or cries at the edge of a chasm? I wish that some

42

spark of me could have jumped that gap. I wish I could have filled my daughter with something of my own that would have made her live.

But on that night at the end of January, Anna did live. She was in critical condition, but stable. The nurses said they'd call us if anything changed. "Why don't you get some rest and come back in the morning?"

And then something else happened. I don't recall exactly when — it was only a moment — yet when I think back on it, I am filled with uneasiness.

At some point between when Anna returned from surgery and when we left to go home, I went out of the ICN and down the hall to the very end where there is a coffee machine and another small sitting room for nurses, doctors, or parents. It was in this room, behind a closed and curtained door, where Beth would frequently pump her breasts, or we would talk with our doctors, or just sit for a while alone. In any case, for a reason I don't precisely remember, I went down there, probably to get a cup of coffee or our coats. The door was closed, and when I parted the curtains, I saw a couple inside, two parents that we had seen before in the ICN, strangers with whom we had exchanged glances of concern and sympathy, but nothing more. In the waiting room they were sitting on the plastic-covered couch. Their knees were together, and the upper part of their bodies hung over one another like willow trees weighted with ice. They were all limbs, tangled hair, and Kleenex in clenched hands. They were sobbing in low catching sounds. So I let the curtain close and went back into the ICN where I held my daughter's hand.

Later we saw them leaving through the double doors, the woman in a wheelchair, the man pushing, and one of the sisters from pastoral care patting the woman's wrist. We didn't say good-bye, or sorry, and we never saw those people again. I can hardly recall their faces, their clothes, or even their approximate age. At some level, I know I tried to ignore them, or tried to wipe them from the realm of possibility. Yet now I remember the curving shape of their bodies. I feel their weighted limbs.

October 23

Yes, I know that two days ago Anna would have been nine months old, longer in the world than she was in the womb. But it is getting harder now to imagine what she would have been like. It is as though my mind is stuck with her in the past. I see her right now as I saw her then. When I think of her older than when she died, all I can do is extrapolate from what I actually knew. I can't really see the surprises. I can't hear her first words. I can't hear her sing. I can't feel in my gut the loss of her innocence.

Today I don't like this imagining of what she might have been. It feels fake, presumptuous, like a trick of the mind, as though I can go right along, watching her grow, re-creating her life, as though she hadn't actually died.

But I will go on speculating — I'm sure of that. I will imagine seeing her someday, a reedy kid in a pack of teenagers. Or I will think of her, years from now, holding a child of her own.

I know that in writing this I am trying in some way to bring Anna back to life. And I know in the end that that is impossible. But what else do you do? Where else do you turn? Where do you pour out your fatherhood when your only child is dead?

October 24

Even as we have been trying to get another child going on our own, we have been thinking about adoption. I am thirty-six; Beth will be thirty-nine this December; and many adoption agencies will not consider any parent beyond the age of forty. So there is the pressure of time, a pressure that somehow feels like a violation, like a threat to my connection with Anna. I flip through adoption manuals and see faces of children that are not my own. My heart goes out to some of them, like another little girl with Tetralogy of Fallot. Yet I can't envision myself as her father. It seems too early for any of this.

It seems that my love is a finite thing, and just now I don't have enough to spare.

October 25

During the last three late-afternoons, I have been raking up acorns in the yard. Out back we have one towering white oak in the center of the lawn and another in the near corner. The backyard is small, about thirty by forty feet, but already I have filled more than thirty shopping bags with these hard brown nuts, each with a wormy pinkish white root, an inch or two long, coming out of the pointed end. In any given square foot of lawn you could find hundreds of them burrowed into the grass, the little root twisting down for soil. When you rake them up, they resist and finally break away. Or often you have to get down on your hands and knees, working your fingers through the grass to find them and pull them out.

I have never seen anything like it, the sheer number of them. They're all over the neighborhood, filling birdbaths and gutters, kids kicking them down the sidewalks. I have never had to rake them up before, and I suppose I could have left them in the grass to rot or grow, shearing off the seedlings next spring with the mower. But there were so many of them. They smothered the grass, and when you went out back it was like walking on marbles.

So why this terrific fecundity and waste: thirty bags lined up on the floor of our garage, thousands of seeds, their white roots searching? Though I know it isn't so, it feels like a mockery. It is the harvest time. All these acorns, apples, seeds, and gourds. Such careless fruitfulness when a child is gone.

October 30

We could barely afford it, but last Thursday we flew to Minnesota to join Beth's family for her father's retirement party. Over the weekend we spent some time with Beth's sister and brother-in-law,

Ann and Dan, and their four-month-old girl, Libby. Libby was born on June 27, the day that Anna was admitted to the hospital for her heart surgery; and I remember talking with Ann and Dan on the phone soon after: trying to share with them the birth of their child and the death of our own. So in my mind, Libby and Anna are inextricably bound. One arrived as the other departed. They would have been cousins, contemporaries, and probably friends, though you could tell they would have been very different kinds of people.

I realize that when I hold other children, I am always remembering, comparing. I am as proud and biased as any father. When I hold Libby I feel fourteen pounds of chunky energy. She is wonderfully strong and vigorous. She rolls over. She sits. With help, she even takes little steps, dances, and when you put her over your shoulder, she arches her neck and back, like a powerful diver.

How different Anna was. So much lighter, more slender, her body willowy, pliant, her movements delicate, as though from some deep awareness of her own fragility. Anna's life was in her eyes, that wide-open watchfulness, darting, alert; and behind them a tight-wired thing, stretched and pegged, a high humming that you could only feel.

Of course I am exercising my parental bragging rights, yet I believe what I say. Anna was small. Because of her heart condition, her physical development was slightly delayed. She could have been stronger, more energetic. But if you had met her and held her, I think you would have liked her. Her life was like the thinnest and livest of wires. I think you would have felt that at the center of your heart.

October 31

Halloween. Dusk. The smell of rain. Damp leaves along the sides of the road, the cars whisking them.

Last night I carved the pumpkin: the wide oval eyes and mouth, horrified, like a Munch painting. Now it sits on the porch railing, glowing with candlelight. I have two bowls of candy: one filled with shining Hershey's Kisses, the other a tangle of lollypops with Tootsie

Rolls at the core. Two kids in gorilla outfits have just roared by on skateboards. It is nearly dark. Beth will be home soon. From a ways up the block, I can hear children's voices, little shrieks and hoots, and I will go upstairs and turn on the light in Anna's room.

November 1

A postscript on Halloween.

Batman costumes are all the rage this year, though still there are plenty of fairies, princesses, clowns, cowboys, and Draculas. In this neighborhood, teenage boys like to be transvestites, prisoners, or punk rockers, their hair in purple spikes. And one trio of high school girls — how can I not mention this? — they stood on our doorstep with ribbons in their hair, pacifiers in their mouths, their gangly bodies in pink leotards and sagging diapers made out of sheets. "We're babies! Trick or treat!" — all giggles and hormones. In spite of it all, you have to laugh. How can you help it?

One mother actually did bring her baby, a five-week-old, while she was escorting her son, a weary vampire, around the neighborhood. She lives a few blocks away. We don't really know her, but she must have seen us pushing Anna around in the stroller last spring and summer.

She was standing at the bottom of our porch stairs, holding the infant, as her son took a lollipop from the bowl. "How's your baby?" she asked me right out of the blue.

It was a well-meaning question we often run into, especially from people we hardly know. You don't want to tell the truth, and you don't want to lie. You have to say something, but you don't want to get into it. It is invariably awkward.

"It's a sad story" was about all I could say. "She didn't live."

You could see the woman wince with the same uneasiness that I also was trying to hide. She shook her head slowly, and for an instant I had the distinct impression that there was some unspeakable sadness in her own life as well. She was young, she held a child, but her eyes

47

were empty and pouched. Where was her husband? Was there a husband? Why did she have an infant outside, without even a hood or hat, on a damp windy night like this?

"I'm sorry," she replied, and we stood there sort of shrugging as the boy went back down the stairs and held her free hand. We all said Happy Halloween — it was a night of imaginary horrors. Then they turned up the sidewalk toward the neighbor's house where cardboard skeletons hung in the windows.

November 2

Something barely perceptible has happened, something we haven't talked about, and something good perhaps, though I'm not sure that I like it.

Two weeks ago, we had a mason come over to give us an estimate for repairing the cracks and leaks in our chimney. Just before the man arrived, I folded up Anna's Swyngomatic that had stood on the hearth since her death and took it into the back study where I leaned it, still folded, against the bookshelves there. I didn't think too much about it then; nor, when the man finished examining the fireplace, did I feel it necessary to return the swing to the living room and set it up again on the hearth. Instead, it has stayed right there against the shelves. We haven't mentioned it. It hasn't seemed like a big deal. Yet it was the first time in four months that I had actually moved something of Anna's, folded it up, and put it slightly out of the way, as though she wouldn't be needing it for a while.

Perhaps this is the way that grief subsides, or changes — these little disturbances, movements of furniture, clothes pushed to the back of a drawer. But if this is healing, then why does it feel like an act of forgetting, or an abnegation, a literal pushing aside of that which helps you remember? Is the price of healing a loss of memory? Or a callousness?

I suppose it is necessary and inevitable, yet the idea of carrying her things down to the basement still makes me cringe. I need these mementos. I am afraid of forgetting, though of course I forget every day. Here and there a detail, a date. Or even the exact sound of her cry.

How in the world could that already be gone? Where are my ears? My eyes? Hands? Her lashes were long and dark, her eyebrows soft and wispy. Yes, I have that. I'm sure of it. Even as I feel her sliding away.

November 3

Tomorrow Anna will have been dead for four months. It still seems impossible, so cruel — she should be crawling around in the playpen. And now it strikes me that on a day next month, just before Christmas, Anna will have been dead for longer than she was alive. Day by day our time without her is layering over our time with her, like these oak leaves covering the grass in the backyard. I rake them up, and they keep on falling. The grass goes thin and dormant. So what will it mean when the first snow comes? Or a glaze of ice? Or in the spring, when the new shoots come out of the ground?

November 6

We came into the ICN early on the morning of February 1, the day after Anna's colostomy and tracheal surgery, and she was still on the elevated tray beneath the heat lamp, her chest going up and down with the respirator. She was still unconscious, sedated, her arms outstretched. She had had a shaky night, and the nurses and doctors had been tinkering with IV medications and the dials on the respirator. Angela was already at work, impossibly awake, taking blood samples every half hour. There was still some concern about Anna's blood CO_2 level (and some other level that I can't recall), but she seemed to be holding her own. Her heart was performing well. She was urinating, little spouts of yellow liquid that meant that her kidneys were doing OK.

So we waited in that preoccupied, nervous way that you wait at bedsides. You straighten sheets or a wisp of hair. Beth started knitting a pair of sea-green booties. I tended to talk, babble, ask questions, or just keep moving, shuttling from one side of Anna's crib to the other, running after doctors in the hall.

I don't have now, and I don't think I had then, during those first days after her surgery, a sense that at any specific moment Anna had suddenly "turned a corner." It was less dramatic than that, so gradual were the initial increments of her recovery, and so fraught were they still with the possibilities of danger. From one day to the next, they were able to cut down the percentage of oxygen she required from the respirator. Then late on February 2, the respirator was removed from her throat, and she was breathing on her own beneath a big plastic hood that went over her head and shoulders like an oversized helmet for an astronaut or a deep-sea diver. Slowly they weaned her of more oxygen, and I remember holding through the portal of the hood, a kind of fancy atomizer that humidified the air she breathed, soothing her throat and lungs. By the end of the next day, she was breathing room air. She was beginning to emerge from a snow of morphine. Her color was better. She was still splayed out, vulnerable and naked; but on her feet now were those sea-green booties, tied on with ribbons, something light and playful about them, as if she was getting ready to dance.

November 7

During all this time, Beth's mother, Betsy, had stayed at our house, holding that part of our lives together so we could spend our days in the hospital. In the meantime, Carl, Beth's dad, was arranging various business trips with stopovers in Washington so he also could spend some time here. On the night of February 3 or 4, during a lull at the ICN, we were finally able to bring them in to see their first grandchild for the first time. Anna was up on the tray, sedated, but that hardly mattered. All the wires and tubes in the world can't lessen a single human presence, or the will of others to see beyond and through them. Beth's parents looked at Anna for a moment, and then I remember them reaching out and touching her hair.

At any number of times like that during Anna's life, I felt a kind of fullness or engagement that I could never have imagined before I was a father. It was not like feeling peaceful, or satisfied, or particularly happy. In fact, I felt it even as we held Anna as she was dying. More than anything else, it was like being wholly alive, every atom of body and mind reaching toward one particular thing with the absolute certainty that where you are and what you are doing — no matter what the outcome — is right.

Now I miss that feeling: my sure place in the world as I bent over that tray and stroked Anna's skin. I don't know how long it would have lasted, or how much it depended upon the extremity of her need. I don't know what I would have felt when she had wholly recovered, or when, inevitably, she would have gone off on her own.

Still, I wish I could have found out.

November 8

On the morning of February 5, when we came into the ICN, Anna had been moved from the elevated tray and back into her familiar isolette. She had had three good days in a row. The nurses had removed the plastic tubes in her sides that had drained off fluid in her chest cavity. She was still hitched up to all the monitors. She was groggy, but she was beginning to open her eyes.

That day was my thirty-sixth birthday, and surely my happiest. It was also the first day in almost a week that we could hold Anna again in our arms.

November 9

Given the retrospective nature of this, and what has happened since, it may be difficult for me to convey a real sense of the anticipation and excitement of those next two weeks. Anna got better and better, faster than the doctors had expected, and there was that feeling that would recur at other times in her life that suddenly and strangely she was taking things into her own hands. You could see it in her face, all bright and alert, "our miracle baby" the nurses were calling her, and some, including a few doctors, were openly doubting the severity of her heart condition. How could her heart be working inefficiently when she was looking this good? She should have been bluer, more ashen. Even the cardiologists were somewhat befuddled. "We'll wait and see," they said.

On February 7, Beth's mother held Anna in the rocking chair in the ICN before catching a cab to the airport and flying home to Minnesota. Then later that day, Dr. Hoy said that Anna was doing so well that they would move her, still in her isolette, across the hall to the Intermediate Nursery, a step down from the ICN.

This was happy news, something we had been hoping for, but when it actually came, catching us by surprise, we didn't know just what to feel. Until then Anna had lived her entire life in the ICN, and we had spent the most important part of our lives there too. We knew all the nurses, the doctors, and medical procedures. I can still hear the deep heavy roll of the X-ray machine, and see on my daughter's narrow chest the dark X, like two cross hairs in a window of light. I learned how to accept that, and to walk out of that room despite Anna's cries, then to come back in after the X ray, and hold her again.

I am not exaggerating in saying that the ICN was the place where Anna was given her life through the hard work of good people. It was also a place where I think I learned about patience, care, my wife's strength, my own dependence, the relative smallness of my endeavors, and our capacity to love a child. It is hard to leave a place like that, even to go across the hall. It was a big move, all new terrain. It was the first time in Anna's life that she was out of intensive care and out of immediate danger.

November 11

4:00 A.M.: Often I can't sleep, or rather, I fall asleep after reading for a while, and then a few hours later I am up thinking, or remembering, or just listening to whatever comes through our bedroom window, which we keep partly open, even as the weather is getting colder.

I don't have the sense, when I awaken, that I have been dreaming of Anna. It is somehow different than that, more palpable, a lingering thing, like the actual smell of her on the sheets where some mornings we'd lie her between us. For the first few weeks after her death, I was sleepless with the images of her death itself, the wonder and horror of that. It was such a small part of her life — the dying part — but I couldn't get it out of my head. Now that seems to have receded some, and I am awakened more to that smell than to any particular image. There is a terrific sadness to it, instead of the horror. It fills the room: part urine, part sweat, part Baby Magic shampoo, part sweet and soured milk, all mixed with the scent of my own tiredness, a warm and rich humidity.

There is nothing like a child, or the death of one, to awaken you to the feel of this time of night. I hear long freight trains rumbling north and south along the Route 1 corridor. I hear the big engines, a few miles away, churning over the trestle and then the whistle at the crossing at Bladensburg Road. Now the sound trails off, and there are crows ruffling up high in the pin oak out front. It is cold in the house. No cars on the road. About an hour ago when I came downstairs, bleary-eyed, I got into my sweatshirt and sweatpants. I put on water for coffee, let out the dog, and stood on the back porch. There was a full moon out, and the yard was still and shiny. You could smell the frost and the withered leaves. They were almost all down; the oaks were bare, the sky wide and silver. Along the fence to the right, though, I could see Anna's new tree, just as lush as the day I planted it. It was standing in the dark pool of its own shadow. It looked exotic, out of place, out of season. It hadn't lost a leaf; it hadn't even turned. And when I went out there and touched it, its branches were pliant, its leaves soft in the hard frost.

It is in these delicate things where hope resides. In the persistence of what is fragile. It awes and frightens me, this dogwood — such tender fullness at this time of year.

November 13

I want to mention an infant boy, Abdu, and his mother, whose name I will probably never know, though for three weeks we shared with her a kind of intimacy in the ICN. Abdu was in the isolette that adjoined Anna's. He was very premature, born perhaps at twenty-eight or thirty weeks, just after his lungs had developed and his eyes had barely opened. When we first met him, he wasn't much longer than the length of your hand, a beautiful child with heavy black hair, dark deep-set eyes, and the most remarkable chiseled face, as though he was already a young and sensitive man. He was there when Anna came into the ICN, and he was there when she left. Each afternoon or evening, his mother would come in to be with him, sometimes twice, for three or four hours. She was a striking woman of African descent, tall, mocha-colored. She wore long black skirts, a turban, and wide intricately patterned scarves. She would sit on a stool, peering through the plastic, with both of her elbows on the edge of the isolette. Directly across from her, we would be looking in at Anna, and through the plastic of both isolettes, as through a number of windows, we could see her looking at her own sick child, and sometimes glancing up — so much sadness and hard hope in her face.

For the first day or so, we didn't speak with her, though soon we began exchanging pleasantries, which evolved into a small sort of visiting ritual. We would go over and look at Abdu, and she would come over and look at Anna. We said all those things that you say about babies, their cuteness, their little arms and legs. We learned all about Abdu's treatment, his brady spells, and his mother got an earful from us. Sometimes when we came in, if she was already there, she would tell us how Anna was doing, whether she had been asleep or awake, crying or comfortable. Then when she would leave for the night, one of us would occasionally find ourself checking in on Abdu, chatting with his nurse; and once I recall moving the heart monitor on top of his isolette, turning it just a little, so we could see it from where we were sitting with Anna.

November 14

On the day that Anna was tranferred from the ICN to the Intermediate Nursery, Abdu's mother hadn't yet arrived, so I left a note on his isolette that said "Good Luck." I signed our names, then "Anna's parents" in parentheses. Over the next ten days, we saw her sporadically in the halls, her long skirt flowing across the linoleum. We said hello and asked about each other's babies, but we never again exchanged a glance like the ones through the walls of our isolettes. In fact, we only saw her once again, and that by chance, about four and a half months later in the Georgetown Pediatric Clinic. I had Anna over my shoulder. Beth and I were taking her into the cardiologist's examination room when I saw the woman in her familiar turban and scarf, standing at the receptionist's desk. She was holding Abdu in her arms. He looked healthy, handsome, and he was bigger than Anna by then. We held the babies so they could look at each other. We remarked on how adorable they were. I think Anna started crying then, the nurse was waiting, and so we waved and scooted on down the hall.

There is no way that Abdu's mother could know that Anna has died, though somehow I feel a vague need to tell her — not enough to make me do anything about it, but just enough to keep feeling it now and then. She is probably one of those people that we will never see again, and I doubt she's thought very much about us. Still I have this feeling that if we ever run into her somewhere, some-time, and we tell her that Anna has died, she will be one of those people who really understands, who feels it all the way to the bottom.

As for Abdu, I hope he is well. He should be sitting up in a high chair by now, cereals and pureed vegetables all over the tray and floor. I hope he lives to take this life whole, to feel love and joy and sadness, to see his own children born, grown; and one day to lean over his mother's bed, to feel in his hands the force of her life. He will have that look in his eyes that we saw in hers.

November 17

And one more thing, one more note about the nurses in the ICN. At 1:00 P.M. on Saturday, July 8, four days after Anna died, we had a small memorial service for her in the chapel at Georgetown Hospital. There were friends, colleagues, a number of Anna's doctors, and our families. Beth and I would say a few words, as would some friends and my sisters; and Beth's brothers would play some music. About five minutes before we were to begin, Beth and I were still welcoming people at the door, when they came around the corner, four or five of them, almost as we had seen them coming down another hall, months before, pushing Anna in her isolette after her successful surgery. They had come straight from the ICN, still in their blue scrubs and elastic booties: some of those nurses who had cared for Anna.

Two days before, I had had that phone conversation with Angela, and though she had to be away for the weekend, she must have put a note on the door of the ICN, announcing that Anna had died and that there would be a memorial service.

What more can I say about this, or what precisely it means? This morning I read in the paper about six Jesuit priests and two others tortured and murdered by death-squads in El Salvador. I read of another "drug related" killing in the dark holes of D.C., and a woman who last Monday stabbed her three sons to death (ages three, four, and five) in a "quiet suburban neighborhood north of Baltimore." Then I think of those nurses, their gentle hands in the isolette, the blue ripple of their scrubs as they came around the corner to embrace us, people they hardly knew, and then to sit for an hour and remember our daughter.

November 18

Compared to the ICN, the Intermediate Nursery (or Nursery D) was like some slow-paced resort for the elderly. The lights were dimmer. Nurses wore white, the walls a creamy beige. There were draw-curtains on the windows, a few magazines on the counters beneath the oxygen ports; and in the air, often that soft nudge of another world: a radio playing low, "Easy Listening," "Soft Rock." And to think, this was Anna's introduction to music.

"If we can only get her home." We must have said it every night when we returned from the hospital. "If we can only get her in this door and close it behind us. . . ."

On February 8, when Anna was nineteen days old, she swallowed something for the first time in her life: a barium solution that was filmed as it went down her throat. Later that day, Beth and I went into a small dark office with Dr. Hoy where we saw the film projected against a fluorescent background. It was a two- or three-minute clip, but more exciting for me than any full-length movie. For there you could see the liquid going into Anna's mouth, her jerky swallowing movements, peristaltic action. And there, right there — he reversed the film and made it go slowly — you could see it passing though a small, slightly narrowed part of her throat, the mended part, like sand moving swiftly through an hourglass. There was no leakage. The liquid continued on to her stomach. This meant that Anna could begin taking some food orally: first a clear bottled solution called Pedialyte, then mother's milk in monitored amounts, and then at long last, she could breast-feed.

November 20

11:15 P.M.: Right now we are in the midst of a big windstorm, and the electricity is out, the house lit with candles. The gusts are up to sixty miles per hour, they are saying on the radio. So stay indoors. Don't drive unless you absolutely have to, and if you are on the road, avoid all bridges.

Well, I'm not about to go driving, but how can I resist going outside on a night like this?

Out back the oaks are swaying, back and forth, maybe fifteen feet at the very top. The neighborhood is dark, except for the starlight.

Leaves swirl in the air. The neighbor's wind chime is riotous, and otherwise, all you hear is the roar of the storm, like the ocean, or when, as a kid, you'd cup seashells up close to your ears and hear the surf breaking inside your head.

In a way, Anna's death has been like that, like a caged wind between my ears, coming in gusts, but without any sound, just the long hard push of it. In the dim light of our backyard, I could see an oak limb, about ten feet long, that had been torn down and shattered on the lawn. The outermost branches still had a few leaves, spinning and rattling in the wind.

November 21

That branch on the lawn. A lost limb.

At 3:00 A.M. on Saturday, July 2, two days before Anna died, our doctors made a last-gasp effort to save her life. Something mysterious had hit her after her successful heart surgery. Her kidneys had shut down. She retained fluid, doubling her body weight, and nothing in the world could make her urinate. The day before, they had tried a passive dialysis machine, a sort of filter or artificial kidney, with tubes (cannulas) inserted into the femoral artery of Anna's right leg. It worked, but not well enough. So the doctors conferred, and Dr. Hopkins, our cardiac surgeon, told us there was one more thing they could try, a procedure that had never been done before at Georgetown, if anywhere else. They could remove the passive dialysis machine and hook up (using the same cannulas in her leg) an ECMO, or heart-lung, machine with a larger dialysis component in the middle of the circuit. The ECMO machine would augment the power of Anna's own mended heart in pumping her blood more rapidly through the dialyzer and thus removing more excess fluid, while perhaps allowing her kidneys to rest and reactivate.

There were risks, of course, but it was the only alternative if Anna was to live for more than a few more hours. This was new territory. There was the possibility of hemorrhaging and brain damage if the machine caused her blood pressure to go up too high. As always, there was the danger of infection. And one more thing, a significant but small risk in relation to the weight of her life: because the machine would take blood from her femoral artery, the blood flow to the rest of her leg would be reduced. In the end, if Anna survived, she could lose her right leg, or some part of it, or perhaps the leg would be stunted, or shorter.

Indeed, as the next twenty-four and thirty-six hours played themselves out, Anna's leg turned purple and black, twice its size, the same leg that I had always held when I had her over my shoulder. It was horrific, almost unbearable. But if Anna had lived, I know I would have had something to tell her, and something to share with her that few other fathers could offer.

For I was born with a dislocated right hip and malformed femur, which were partially corrected through a series of experimental surgeries beginning when I was ten months old. I didn't walk until I was three. I was in a body cast, in and out of the hospital. Even now my right leg is slightly stunted, an inch shorter than my left. My muscles there are smaller. My right foot is smaller. I wear a lift in my shoe and walk and run with a limp that I am usually unaware of.

In the large scheme of things, I am a very lucky man. And perhaps, if Anna had survived, she would have been less fortunate than me. Still, I think I would have understood whatever disability she might have had. I would have felt her fear and embarrassment. I would have told her that despite the terrible unfairness and devastation of this world, she must never give up or despair. I would have told her that the measure of life is not the length of your limbs, but the depth of your heart. That what is truly lived is what is earned. And what is loved is willed, is cut from stone. And that, if anything, will last.

If there was any sense in this world — any reason at all — then Anna should have lived, and I should have been her father, Beth her mother. I will never understand why she died.

Today Anna would have been ten months old, the age I was when (on December 7, 1953) my hip was first operated on. I haven't thought much about this before, yet I think I now know what my

59

parents must have felt when I was wheeled down to surgery, and when years later I took my first steps.

November 22

Maybe my parents, too, were thinking of that part of their lives when they visited Anna for the first time on February 11. It was also the first time we fed Anna mother's milk in a bottle. And it was the day she was taken from her isolette and put in one of those plastic bassinets, open to the air, just like any other normal, healthy baby.

My parents are an unlikely couple. My mother is a strong woman, patrician, passionate, a private-school teacher, her face sharp, jaw set, hair silver, blue eyes hard and soft at the same time. As my father says, she is "always on the go" to one meeting or another, to school, to friends', shopping, church. Her medium is activity. She is dedicated to her children. Her love is hard and deep. When something has to be done, she simply does it efficiently, effectively. That is how she has made her life.

My father has had a harder time with the world and lately with his own health. He is a diffident, caring man who loves his children. He likes to talk about the old days, when railroads were clean, the brass polished, and he was a young businessman with sleek black hair, the heir to his father's prospering linen importing operation in New York. When his father died, however, it all crumbled beneath him. Cotton replaced linen. The New York office was closed up, and for thirty years my father nursed what remained of the business at a small desk in a dark basement corner of our suburban house in New Jersey. Now he is seventy-four, his hair thin, gray, and the grass has long since covered his narrow vegetable garden in the backyard. He has chronic leukemia, high blood pressure, a bad back, and his hands shake.

I must have been a hard son for him to have. I know I was often arrogant, spiteful. We've had our differences. Yet there he was on that day in February, holding Anna. His hands were trembling, but he had her firmly. He held her up tight to his chest with his nose in her hair. In that moment I felt more between us, myself and my father, than I had felt in a very long time. He really wanted to hold Anna, and I really wanted him to hold her. For there must have been a time when he held me like that, and I must have felt as comfortable as my own daughter did in his arms.

There is much that is incomplete or unresolved between my father and me, as there is, I suppose, between most fathers and their sons. There are things we don't talk about, that are best unsaid. As I have grown older, become a father myself, he has grown shy and afraid of my judgment, and I am uneasy about this as well. Still, I love him; he loves me. Sitting there in the Intermediate Nursery with Anna in his arms, I know we both felt it like a change in the air: that regret for what is unattained in our lives, and yet a sudden joy that there was this.

November 23

We are off to my parents' home for Thanksgiving, and from there to New Hampshire to meet old friends, Todd and Robinanne, with whom we had lost touch until a few months after Anna's birth. It was then, last March, that Robinanne called to say they had just had a baby — a girl, whose name was Anna.

November 28

How strange to call another child by the name of your own, though in fact it wasn't as painful as I feared. This Anna is big and blonde with a small, delicate mouth that reminded me of our Anna, as did her eyes, which, though smaller, were wildly alert. She was not in the mood to have strangers holding her, and perhaps that was easiest on us all. I did, however, carry her in a backpack when we went out for a walk in the woods. Our Anna never grew large enough to sit up in a backpack, though she did spend some time in a Snugli, bundled up and strapped to my front, as I'd walk briskly around the neighborhood, keeping her moving until she'd calm.

When we were out in the woods with Todd and Robinanne,

there was a dusting of snow on the ground and the pine boughs. The trail wound over a knoll of young birches and hemlocks, past beaver-chewed trunks, an overturned canoe, to the edge of a wide vlei, studded around with cattails, frozen over and covered with snow — a vast openness, pure and untracked. The air was still, and you could smell the balsam. Todd stomped on the ice. It seemed secure, but we didn't go out there. We stayed on the edge, on the brittle, tufted grass where you knew that nothing could happen.

All along, I felt the weight of their Anna on my back and shoulders. Though I couldn't see her, there was that fine tension of her alertness. She wasn't moving, but I could tell she was awake. Then as we were heading back, as we came into the clearing near the old farmhouse, I felt that moment almost as I had felt it with our own Anna: when a child's body goes limp and relaxed, the breath slows, your own breath slows, and something inside of you slides away.

November 30

As though it was waiting for us to leave, Anna's tree turned color while we were away. The leaves are still attached, still supple, but they are now a deep maroon, like wine left at the bottom of a glass. The red, pink, and white impatiens that we planted around the tree have long since been killed by frost, as have the peonies, daylilies, and hydrangeas. They are all tan husks and stalks. For the moment at least, Anna's tree is the most brilliant thing in the yard. Not a single leaf has fallen.

I have just brought in today's mail, and I see that Anna's final autopsy report has arrived: a large brown envelope with Dr. Hopkins's return address. Its gummed flap is glued and sealed, the metal fastener pushed through the hole, its wings splayed and flattened.

Over the past five months, I have come to better know what will break my heart, and this, I suspect, is one of those things. I am alone in the house. It is late afternoon. I will not open this now. Instead, I will go out for a run, exhaust myself, take a shower. Then when Beth gets home from her aerobics class, when there's water boiling for spaghetti in the kitchen, we'll sit on our family room couch, the curtains pulled, and try to read it.

December 1

Since Anna died, many of our friends and family have said that the death of a child is unimaginable — and they are right. What's strange, and what they probably don't know, however, is that even after it's actually happened, after I've held her body in my arms and kissed her cold gray skin, even as I read and reread this "Report of Pathologic Examination" ("This 5-month old white infant . . . expired at 8:35 A.M. on 7/4/89"), even now it is still unimaginable, perhaps even more unimaginable than it was when she was alive. I just can't get my mind around it, or hold it. It is so much beyond me that a young live thing is gone. Expired.

Of course I understand the concept, an idea expressed by a word, a collection of letters, or a matrix of dots that's called a "report." But in that part of my being where I mostly live, she doesn't seem *gone* or *expired*, and yet she doesn't seem *alive* or *here* either.

I wish I could believe in this thing called heaven. I wish I could know I would hold Anna again. Once a month we meet with a group of parents who have lost children, some of whom speak of the comfort that comes with their belief that they will be with their children in another place. "My Jeffrey is up there," a woman says, pointing toward the acoustic tiles, and she seems to know this in the way that I know that this is a keyboard, and this the letter A. But to meet Anna again, or even for our "spirits" or "essences" to mingle — all this is as incomprehensible to me as her death itself.

I'm afraid I can't understand that she's gone — really gone — and nor can I believe in some kind of afterlife or a place she might be. My mind says she's nowhere, and yet I seem to be searching. The closest thing I can say is that it feels as if she's lost, that she's not to be found, though she isn't very far away.

December 2

Last night we went to what was called a nondenominational candlelight service in memory of children who have died. It began with a priest who, in what I thought were the most patronizing tones, assured us that there was an afterlife, a heaven, that our children, in dying, had undertaken a journey, "like a voyage across an ocean," where there was worldly sadness on one shore, and a welcoming God, hands outstretched, on the other. He said we must believe this, that "there are no atheists in the trenches," that there would be a glorious reunion. He held a globe in his hand and said that dying children spin out of the world by some sort of centrifugal force and then become stars. He said that the end of grief is a resolution through faith. He said we must be grateful to God for bringing these children into the world. He said nothing, though, about a God who, if He has given, has brutally taken away. He said nothing about *why* God might have done this. And he said nothing at all about the cost of death to the children themselves, what it meant to them to be torn from this world, and for some of them to die with excruciating pain.

Where is the resolution in that? And for that matter, why this need for resolution at all? Why the calm after a horror? Why try to make right of what you know is unacceptable? Why not live with the love, and the ashes, too, in your mouth?

That priest. He calls himself a father. He is well-meaning; he is so sure of his ways; but what can he really know about this?

There is nothing so transparent as a want of authority, and nothing so moving as the real thing. When the priest sat down, a woman whose son had died read the names of the parents in attendance, each followed by the name of the child they had lost. Then the woman lit a candle, and as the flame passed one to the other, each parent said the name of his or her child, until all the candles were lit. For a time the room wavered and glowed, and then we extinguished the candles. Now I think of those chiseled names on the black wall of the Vietnam Memorial, or any list of the dead. All those names. Any single name.

I write Anna Loizeaux. I know of nothing more simple and powerful than that.

December 4

Yesterday afternoon a bitter cold front came through, and this morning the backyard is rock hard, little mounds here and there where the ground has heaved.

I'm not sure why I keep going over and over this autopsy report, as if I can find something here that I can really hold on to. It is twelve pages long: first a pathologic diagnosis, then a brief medical history of Anna, a gross pathologic report, a micropathologic report, a small microbiology section, a summary, and finally references. Anna's body and all of her organs are minutely examined and described. It shook us when we first read it a few evenings ago, and it shakes me up now. It brings back all the terror of that last week: Anna lying there, her eyes swollen shut, all the IVs pumping, the orange heat lamp, her mottled leg, the heft of the respirator, her colostomy bag filling with blood, so much going wild and wrong, and still her squeezing our fingers so hard.

Several weeks ago, I wrote that the memories of Anna's last week had "receded some." That was true then, though what I failed to foresee was how powerfully they could resurface. For I realize I am still fearing her death, now, today, exactly five months after it happened. I feel all of her fragility, and somehow I am responding to it in the same way that I did when she was alive. I am reading and rereading the reports, scouring the dictionary and conversion tables. At twenty-eight hours postmortem she weighed approximately 7.8 kilograms, or 17 pounds, almost double her normal weight. Her "crown-heel length" was measured at 63 centimeters, or 24.5 inches, two-thirds of a yardstick. Her "occipito-frontal circumference" (I'll call it her hat size) was 42.5 centimeters or 16.5 inches. I cut a string at that length and make it into a circle on top of my desk. It seems about right, a little big because of the swelling, but almost exactly the size of the circle described by my hands when I touch thumb to thumb and middle finger to middle finger.

That was the shape of her head, and all of this — heart, trachea, lungs, stomach, small and large intestine, mesentery, liver, spleen, pancreas, kidneys, ureters, cloaca, uterus, ovaries, adrenals, thyroid, bone marrow, and brain — all of it was part of her, Anna.

How can I not study this stuff, as though looking for clues, or trying even now to know her better? Her heart weighed thirty grams, or barely an ounce. And while the report doesn't mention how wonderful and wild it was, or how it would fly when I lifted her up and down above my head, it does at least say this: "Scalp hair is brown."

We have a few inches of her hair upstairs in Beth's bureau in a Ziploc bag. The nurse clipped it off and gave it to us when they put an IV in her head just before her heart surgery. When I bring it down here and take it out of the bag, it fills me with so much sadness and remembered joy. It is brown all right, curved like a long S, with a few strands of blonde. It is so thin and fine that in your hand you can hardly feel it.

December 5

You might say this autopsy report is all just data, measurements, observations and remainders of a physical being that do not touch on her spirit or character. I think I even believed this just a few months ago, in September, when we got the preliminary report. I wrote that "this is only the machinery of her," as if I could draw a clear line between what was *her* and what it was that physically made her.

In the end, though, I can't really distinguish her physical being from her character. I can't think of her mischievousness, her joy, her infant courage and will without thinking of her eyes, her hair, and all of her physical frailties. The separation of body and soul is just an idea. I never knew Anna that way (a separate body and soul), and I see no reason to know her that way now. I feel her hair as I felt it then. The shape of her head is the circle of my hands. She had an imperforate anus, and malformed kidneys and ureters. The report notes "bilateral thoracostomy incisions, a patent colostomy with patent mucous fistula in lower left quadrant." She had scars and holes — I can see them all now; I *need* to see them. And I need to remember that none of them stopped her from being happy.

I'm afraid a spirit is not enough to remember. Give me a lock of hair, a length, a weight. I would hold her heart in my hand, if I could.

December 6

In the last analysis, there is no precise medical explanation of Anna's death. There is only a hypothesis without proof, an educated guess that Anna died from complications arising from septic shock (sepsis), or the spread of some massive infection, perhaps originating in her persistant cloaca and traveling up her urinary system or through her fallopian tubes and invading her bloodstream, thus causing her kidneys and then the rest of her organs to shut down.

After all the microbiologic tests, however, no organism could be found. She was on massive pre- and postoperative antibiotics, and there was no evidence of perforation along her gastrointestinal or urinary tracts.

So her death remains a mystery, and it probably always will. We tried to make sure that she had the best doctors, the best care, and even now I am convinced of that. They did all they could do, all anyone could do. Still there is this persistent sense that she should have survived, that if there is meaning in the world, then she was meant to live. There should have been a reason, or something I can point my finger at — even if it's myself — and say with conviction, "*That* is why she died. *That* was it." Instead, my rage and wonder trail into space like smoke in the wind. What do I make of a world such as this?

For the record, this, in medical terms, is how Anna died. I read it again and again, and still I don't altogether believe it.

PATIENT: LOIZEAUX, ANNA   MRUN: 731393   AGE: 5M
PATH #: 89A118   ADMIT DR: HOPKINS, RICHARD A
ADMIT DATE: 06/27/89 SER:SUR/CAR   DISCHARGED:
07/04/89 @ 8:47 AM
REQUESTOR: LOIZEAUX, WILLIAM FATHER
RESTRICTIONS: NONE
AUTOPSY: CARRIAGA, MARISA 07/05/89 1:00 PM 28 HOURS
POST MORTEM
SUMMARY:

This 5-month-old infant with VATER syndrome was admitted to GUH for repair of Tetralogy of Fallot, which was achieved with no intraoperative complications. Cardiopulmonary status was initially stable, but patient subsequently became acidotic and hypotensive with anasarca and acute renal failure. Pulmonary edema and pleural effusions developed and cardiopulmonary status worsened, with thrombocytopenia and gastrointestinal bleeding further complicating the post-operative course. Continuous arteriovenous hemofiltration and extracorporeal membrane oxygenation were begun because of acute renal failure with anuria and poor oxygenation. Despite these efforts, the infant proceeded to bradycardia and asystole and was not resuscitated per parents' request.

As I page through this report once more before putting it away in its envelope, I am again impressed by how hard death must be and what damage it does. Nothing in Anna was spared; all was ravaged. I think of her lying there with our arms around her. I think of all that was happening to her. My poor baby. I hope she didn't feel too much pain. I hope all she felt was our love.

December 7

Yesterday afternoon I spoke with Dr. Hopkins's office and arranged for a meeting on December 19 with him and Dr. Beder, one of Anna's cardiologists, to discuss the final autopsy report and the course of Anna's care. Both doctors suggested the meeting. They want very much to talk with us, and I am surprised by how much I want to see them too. I suspect, when we see them, that Beth and I will learn little that is terribly new or different, but that is probably not the point. Though it will be strange in the hospital without Anna, I think it will feel good to be with these people who worked so hard to keep her alive. They were not unaffected by Anna's life and death. They have sons and daughters of their own.

And perhaps, if there is time while we are at the hospital, we will go over to Cardiac Intensive Care and then to the ICN and say hello to the nurses. I have a powerful urge to go back to these places. I am drawn to them, even if just to look, or to make sure they are still there.

December 8

It is snowing this morning, a fine, light, picking snow that is supposed to get heavier this afternoon, and by evening, we should have half a foot on the ground. While there is hardly an inch out there now, all the schools and many businesses have already been closed. An odd peacefulness has settled outside my windows: the sidewalk empty, only a few cars on the road, their sounds muffled, everything white and transformed.

A little while ago, I went out in the backyard with Jessie. The snow lay on the picnic table, the bench swing, and in the empty bowl of the birdbath. Along the top rail of the fence, on the thin lath of the trellis, and even on our clothesline, it stood impossibly balanced, still and breathless, as though it was painted there. By some delicate adhesion, it caught too on the ribbed leaves of Anna's tree. They are leathery now, still holding on, though they are beginning to curl at the edges, a folding in. A few of them have even turned strangely upward, inside out, cupping the snow like hands.

Later, 11:00 P.M.: I've just returned from an hour or two of cross-country skiing with a friend. I gave him a call, and we met over at the university golf course a few miles from here. The snow had stopped. It was dark of course, but only in that way that it's dark when the moon is hazed, diffuse, and the pale light is reflected all around by snow. You could see almost anything, though only in black and white. There was a starkness to it, a clean crispness, the bare trees like calligraphy.

What you couldn't see, though, was depth and subtlety, those shapes that depend on shadow, texture, or the faint hintings of color. You could be skiing along on what looked like a pure flat whiteness, when suddenly you were tipped downhill, rushing over mounds, through gullies that you had no idea were there.

I am thinking now of those last pages of Joyce's "The Dead." All that snow. And Gretta's memory of Michael Furey, the poor boy shivering beneath the dripping tree. And her grief so many winters later: "I think he died for me." And now Gabriel, her husband, standing at the dim window, his soul swooning, the flakes falling against the lamplight.

I realize that in her life Anna never saw snow. She never felt it in her hair and lashes. She never heard it ticking softly against a window, or against dry leaves; or saw a young man standing outside with his heart in his eyes. Or saw the snow piling on the narrowest twig, balanced there, and felt the wind that takes it away.

December 11

With Anna out of the isolette, there was no plastic between her and us. She was more accessible. We could pick her up and hold her at any time, and as she continued to improve day by day, drinking mother's milk from a bottle, the doctors began removing more of the wires and tubes. Barring any surprises, soon we would be taking her home. We would close our front door behind us, and while surely there would be adjustments and complications, the worst, we thought, was almost certainly over.

On February 13, we met with an "enterostomal therapist" who came up to the Intermediate Nursery and showed us how to remove and replace Anna's colostomy bag, an eight-step procedure that none of us was particularly fond of, though either Beth or myself could do it right now in our sleep. Then, on the following day, Valentine's Day, more than three weeks after her birth, Anna breast-fed for the first time.

Beth, of course, could better tell this part of the story. But what I remember was Anna's urgent groping and finally catching on, drooling as she went, and Beth saying *whooh!* rolling her eyes, wincing, catching her breath, and smiling too. It had been a three-week wait, this moment, for Beth as well — three weeks of determined pumping to keep up her supply for when Anna would need it. I can only imagine what it must have been like for Beth to finally feed her. "It is like being very close," she always said. And what I can't yet imagine is how hard it must have been: to feel her breasts full when Anna had died, and then to pump out her milk all thin and green.

This evening we have bought, put up, and decorated our Christmas tree, a small roundish one, gleaming now with miniature lights. We put it in the same corner of the living room where we had our tree last year, though it wasn't quite so simple as then. For that corner is where Anna's playpen has been, unmoved, since she was alive. We talked about it yesterday, and we decided we'd pack up the playpen and put it down in the basement.

There is no good time to do these things, and yet there is a sad inevitability about it. The tree was here and the playpen was in its way. The present is literally pushing aside the past and packing it downstairs. Something inside of me still cries out at this, even as I unscrew the metal frame and fold the sides and base of it, cushion and all, into its box. Here last spring and summer Anna would lie on her back, cooing and kicking her legs, batting and

71

grasping the bright plastic rings suspended over her head. Or she would spin a four-sided plastic gadget, with a mirror, a dial, and other doo-dads to look at.

Now I am smiling and shaking my head: to think of Anna if she could have seen this tree. How big those eyes, her brows raised, her mouth part open. She would have gazed and gazed.

December 12

On February 16, the doctors removed the big Broviac catheter from Anna's chest. All intravenous feedings and medications had been stopped. A prophylactic oral antibiotic (amoxicillin) was begun at sixty-five milligrams, or one-half of a tablespoon, twice per day. Anna was now cut free of all the monitors and IV lines, all the wires and tubes, except for the gastrostomy tube, which would remain in her stomach for another week, a way of feeding her in case of an emergency. In short, she was on her own, eating, growing, supporting herself.

The long-range plan was to monitor her closely (by weekly appointments), to let her grow, a year if possible, before her heart would have to be mended. Then, if all went well, we would eventually take her up to a doctor in Long Island who had developed a new procedure for rebuilding the lower ends of digestive and genito-urinary systems.

But all of this was in the distant future just then. The next day, we would be taking Anna home. Before she was born, we had set up an old spool crib from Beth's family in the sitting room outside our bedroom door. Beth's mother had made bumpers, and Beth had made cushions for changing tables. On a wicker shelf in the bathroom — it is all still there — we had baby lotion, shampoo, powder, diapers, A and D Ointment, the works.

That night we decided what Anna would wear: a warm, body-length pullover with geese on it, booties, a white sweater and hat my mother had knitted, and a pink and white bunting Beth's mother had sent.

December 13

Before we left the hospital, there were a good number of forms to sign. The nurses filled an entire garbage bag for us with extra diapers, bottles, nipples, colostomy pouches, and various syringes (needleless) for administering Anna's antibiotic or feeding her through her stomach tube. Then we were ready to go. We said good-bye. We stopped at the ICN, and some of Anna's neonatologists and nurses (Susan was on duty, Angela was off) came out to see her.

These moments are often awkward or anticlimactic for me. I don't know what to say that isn't either inappropriate or terribly inadequate. In large measure, these people were responsible for keeping Anna alive, and all we could give them was our gratitude, a bouquet of flowers with a note saying, "Thanks for helping Anna through. Good luck."

Next we rolled Anna down the hall in her plastic bassinet, by the sink and the coat hooks, and then finally through the swinging double doors.

Every once in a while these days, when I am out at the Safeway or Hechinger's, I hear the sound of rolling, pivoting wheels, like the ones on dollies or on the fronts of shopping carts, and I am taken back through those double doors and down the shining hall to the place where Anna was cared for during the first month of her life. I can be standing at the frozen vegetable bin or at the deli counter when this happens. I hear the swiveling wheels beneath her portable isolette, or the ones beneath the frame of her plastic bassinet, and I can almost feel what I was feeling then, as we were rolling her toward home.

I would live those days all over again if it was possible. They were not altogether happy. They were too vital to be happy. But I would live them again — I'd live her whole life all over again — even if I knew what would happen.

A few more inches of snow fell last night, an entirely different texture, thick and gluey. It is weighing down Anna's tree, splaying the limbs like a fan.

December 14

You would think I'd remember everything about our bringing Anna home. I know I drove slowly, like a chauffeur, with Anna in the car seat in the back, and Beth sitting beside her. I know I often looked in the rearview mirror, just to see the quiet satisfaction in Beth's face. The weather was cold and damp. But I don't recall what we talked about as we drove, or if Anna was sleeping. I don't even recall that moment of taking her into the house, despite all its meaning to me now. I can't distinguish it from all the other times that I got her out of the car, still strapped in her plastic seat, took her up the porch stairs, put her down, and fumbled for my keys.

When we got her inside, I probably set her on the dining room table, and one of us must have unstrapped her, pulled her out of the car seat, and maybe we laid her down on the family room couch to take off her heavy bunting. In all her winter clothes (hat, hood, sweater, and bunting), she always looked faintly humorous to me, her arms straight out, all stiff and padded, like those astronauts on the moon. There was a pleasure in seeing her bundled up like this, but a greater pleasure was taking her in from the outside, into a warm familiar room, and seeing her real shape emerge (narrow shoulders, all the hair, ears) as you peeled off the outermost layers. Then you were really getting somewhere, layer by layer, unlocking the feel and smell of her. We must have done that there on the family room couch, then perhaps we took turns holding her, or maybe Beth nursed her and we just sat for a while, getting used to what we were feeling.

December 16

Today was Beth's birthday, this year a low-key affair, a day of remembering and trying to look forward. We spent the afternoon Christmas shopping, had dinner out, and when we came home, we lit candles and she opened some cards and presents. From my mother, she got a set of demitasse cups, and from a friend an old volume of Celtic verse. I gave her a porch swing, which I will sand, assemble, paint

74

with urethane, and hang out on our front porch this spring. It may not be exactly what she's always wanted. That, I'm afraid, has already been lost. Yet I hope that it will be a place where someday we can sit with another child.

December 18

Even as a memory, the feel of our house with Anna in it is as palpable to me as her absence. All last winter and spring, I'd return home about 10:30 each Thursday night after I'd been teaching my class. As I turned into the driveway, I'd see the three dark windows in Anna's dormer and, along the side of the house, the flickering light of the TV behind our family room curtains. I'd know that Anna was asleep and Beth was downstairs, groggy-eyed, watching a mystery. I'd know she'd have the little white monitor on the arm of the couch. I'd know that we'd talk, then I'd go upstairs. I'd look in on Anna, who was quiet, still, and I'd bend over close and hear her breathing.

When I came through the front door, the house always seemed to confirm this scenario. All these things in their places. The basket of kindling. The rocking chair in the corner. The soft mumble of the TV from the back room. Even the cracks in the plaster walls spoke of a kind of assurance, a slow settling of ways. This was as it should be. This was how it was meant to be.

Today the house looks almost the same, though of course it feels very different. This morning Beth slammed out the front door, knocking paint chips off the molding. We had had an argument, the second big one we've had since Anna died — the first (the circumstances of which I can't recall) conveniently omitted from these pages.

It all began with the stupidest of things. I was annoyed that I had to clean salt from the sidewalk off the floors again, a job I had just done yesterday. Beth was annoyed that I was annoyed. Then I thought she was angry at me, and she thought I was angry at her. Then we *were* angry at each other, sniping away, the gist of it being that the other person was less tolerant, less understanding, and besides, the whole thing wouldn't have started if the other one of us hadn't said such and such in such a way. We are both proud. We don't back down. And finally one of us slams out the door. Usually it is me, though this time it was Beth, the paint chips flying.

Now as I look at them, like shards of glass on my clean floor, I am still angry and ashamed, and this house, once filled with Anna's presence, feels so cold and empty.

Later we talk on the phone, and we each take those small steps back toward the center of our lives. We are sorry. We are under stress, bereft, and so far unable to get pregnant again. Still, we can't blame it all on the loss of Anna. We have both been quick on the trigger of late, and I am probably the most combative. There is a taut thing at the heart of me that is very reluctant to bend. In the service of what is right, it is an admirable perseverence, while under other circumstances it is pure stubbornness, a will to have my own way. I am as proud of the one as I am ashamed of the other; and sometimes I think I have a handle on this, when to invest my persistence and when to let it go. But I am still learning.

December 19

I am amazed sometimes by the coincidences we run into. As I have noted, last Saturday, December 16, was Beth's thirty-ninth birthday. It was also the date on which the time since Anna's death (five months, twelve days) became longer than the time that she was alive (five months, eleven days). Finally, it is the one-year anniversary of the fetal ultrasonic scan that first indicated a possible problem.

Because of the history of hip anomalies in my family, our doctors recommended that we follow Anna's (then, "the baby's") growth in utero. We had seen ultrasonic images before. A few years ago when Beth's first pregnancy was ending in a sixth-week miscarriage, we saw on the doctor's screen the enlarged uterus, and then the embryonic sac, a vague elliptic shape, pulsing, like something gathering in the sky. Two days later, after a weekend of cramps and more bleeding, we saw the image again, the same shape, but it was only an outline now, a ring of stars, with nothing pulsing inside.

What we saw of Anna on Beth's birthday one year ago (about a month before she was born) was altogether different. Still, it had the feel of strange forms flowing in the sky. But as Dr. Schruefer moved the transducer over Beth's stomach, he'd stop and point out clearly recognizable features on the screen: the shape of Anna's head, her crossed feet, and a hand held modestly over her genitals. Now and then she would move softly, like someone turning in an easy dream. I remember staring, transfixed, and for an instant I was almost a child again, sitting on rainy days in front of the aquarium in my parents' kitchen, those magical shapes gliding all around.

I could have watched all day, and as it was, we were with the doctor for more than an hour. We saw Anna's heart pumping, her lungs, her bones. Turning little dials and pushing buttons, Dr. Schruefer took measurements, lengths, and circumferences, explaining it all as he went. He is a robust, fatherly man who plays Bach on a tape recorder while he works. He is a bass in a church choir. He has a deep resonant voice. I remember all this because, at a certain point in the examination, when a dark round shape appeared on the screen, he stopped talking and started his low humming along with the music, filling the room as he squinted now at the screen.

That circular shape. He moved the transducer carefully, revealing the shape from a number of angles. It looked like almost a perfect sphere, a ball about the size of a marble, pressing against Anna's bladder, some kind of tumor or cyst, he finally said. He had never seen anything exactly like this before, so we watched it for a long time, watching her small bladder fill and drain. That was good news. Her urinary system was working. But if this mysterious round thing was growing, and if it got big enough to shut off her urinary tract, then she would run out of amniotic fluid and die if she wasn't born.

Otherwise, the examination revealed no other gross abnormalities. From what the doctor could see, her heart looked fine, her kidneys oddly shaped, but functioning, and her hips — after all, that's what we were there to see — were perfect. As for that round growth, it would be monitored at least once every two weeks. The best guess was that it was a fetal ovarian cyst that, if life-threatening, would be removed immediately after an induced labor and birth.

On January 3, we had our next appointment with Dr. Schruefer, and the round "cystlike" shape in Anna's abdomen had grown to the size of a Ping-Pong ball. Though there was still plenty of amniotic fluid, the rate of growth was alarming. There was that clammy, helpless feeling that we would have at other times in her life. On the 9th, we met with Dr. Hoy, the pediatric surgeon who would be on hand at Anna's birth. We went to our regular Wednesday-night birth classes and made sure there was always gas in the car. Meanwhile, as if to reassure us, Anna kept moving in Beth's belly.

Then on the 11th, at another session with Dr. Schruefer, we saw that the round shape, as mysteriously as it had grown, had diminished slightly in size. We weren't out of danger, but you could feel the relief. We even saw a fuzzy image of Anna's face — I have the photo right here in black and white. It is her all right. I can recognize her in utero: her cheeks big, her eyes closed, sleeping; she has a high forehead, and if you look closely you can see, scrunched against the wall of the amniotic sac, her dark mop of hair.

We had another appointment with Dr. Schruefer scheduled for January 25, but Beth's water broke early in the morning of the 21st, and that afternoon Anna was born.

Even now, no one can explain that round shape with certainty, though it may have been a ball of meconium that accumulated in an unusual place because of Anna's strange anatomy. In any event, no ovarian cyst was discovered when Dr. Hoy performed the gastrostomy shortly after her birth. There were many other problems, but there was no round shape. So it must have been absorbed, or expelled, or it disappeared. As with so many things in Anna's life and death, there is no proof, no certainty, no reason.

December 20

We spent most of yesterday afternoon at the hospital, talking with Drs. Beder and Hopkins, and many of Anna's nurses from Cardiac Intensive Care. It was the second time we had been back there since Anna's memorial service. I pulled into the same lot where we always parked when we brought Anna in for her weekly tests and exams. Then we went up to Dr. Hopkins's office where we had brought Anna last May 11 when he saw her for the first time and we discussed her forthcoming surgery.

It is hard, going back to these places, and yet it feels right. Even the smell of the damp winter air, the crunch of salt outside the hospital door, or just the weight of my winter coat — it all took me back, and she was almost present again.

In a yellow conference room we talked to the doctors about her surgery and treatment. We used the past tense when discussing her now; it was different of course; but still there was that effort to figure things out, almost an urgency, and I felt — even though I knew she was gone — that I was doing something for her again.

We all went over the autopsy, and Beth and I had a list of questions: Given the known bacteria in Anna's cloaca, could she have been on a longer or more rigorous regime of preoperative antibiotics? Why didn't the antibiotics, pre- and postoperative, work? Was there any way to sterilize her cloaca? Or could/should her cloaca have been repaired *before* her heart surgery?

We almost knew the answers to these questions before we asked them. A few evenings ago, we read all the articles we could find in the medical library that touch on Anna's virtually unique condition. In the light of all that's presently known, her treatment was unerringly appropriate. Patiently the doctors answered our questions: A long regime of preoperative antibiotics could have bred a superbacteria. Or the antibiotics may not have worked because, in part, the immune system is compromised during heart surgery. And no, the cloaca cannot be sterilized; and her heart, unmended, couldn't have supported her through cloacal surgery.

In the end, they had made all the right judgments. They had

been over and over her case. Anna shouldn't have died, but still she did. What happened was simply beyond them, beyond all effort, will, and present understanding.

As we shook the doctors' hands and walked out of the room, I had that disquieting sense of a chapter closing, or some part of me, like outgrown clothes, being set aside in a closet. In our division of labor during Anna's life, it had usually been my job to talk with the doctors and try to make sure that they were talking to one another about Anna's case. Now again we were talking, and they were talking to one another. And while they said as we left, "Keep in touch," "Don't hesitate to call," it was clear that all of our words had run themselves dry, and this was the place where our talking would end.

This evening we are off to New Jersey to spend Christmas with my parents and my two sisters, their husbands, and kids.

December 23
NEW JERSEY

I have just gotten back from a late-night run, showered, and I am sitting at the end of the dining room table in the house I grew up in. The grandfather clock in the hall says 12:30, so it is actually the 24th, the first hours of Christmas Eve. As I am writing, my mother, in her organized way, is setting out the soup tureen and bowls for tomorrow's meal, watering the centerpiece, and drying all the glasses with Christmas trees on them. Everyone else is in bed, all the kids, my father, my sisters, their husbands, and also Beth. My mother bustles around. It is all so familiar to me: the feel of this house with my sisters asleep, the click and sway of the pendulum, my mother humming as she works, and the smell of Lemon Pledge on the cherrywood table. I am in my bathrobe, pajamas, dead tired, yet my foot keeps bouncing beneath my chair. I realize that once again I am that wired, confused kid in my mother's dustless house. She arranges the candles on the buffet, we say good night, and she goes down the hall to the bathroom. When she comes out, though, she doesn't go straight to bed, but returns to

80

the dining room in her blue robe, bifocals, and ridiculous pink plastic curlers that she'd rather not be seen in. At first she seems to be looking for something, and then she just stands at a loss in the doorway. Her face is soft and somber. She says, "I wish Anna was here." And because we are suddenly on the edge of tears, and because I am too old to crawl into her lap, and because she is not old enough yet to crawl into mine, I can only nod and force a smile. And of course, she knows that.

Together we maintain the illusion of my composure. It is an old habit with us. "Don't work too hard," my mother says from the doorway. "Don't forget to go to bed." Then she locks the doors and shuts out the lights — all but the one I am working by.

On a table in my parents' living room there lies a photo album of Anna that my mother has put together. By and large, it procedes chronologically, beginning with photos of Anna in the ICN and ending with the long basket of flowers that Beth's mother had arranged for Anna's memorial service. It is a nice book to hold in your hand. It is bound in cloth, aqua-blue, and when you open it, the photos on each page are clear and bright behind a skin of shiny plastic. On the first page, my mother has written Anna's name and the dates of her birth and death, and on the last there are passages that Beth and I read at the memorial service. Otherwise, there are no captions or explanations. Your eye glides from photo to photo, about forty in all. When you reach the end I don't know what you'll think, though for me it's almost as if I can hold her life right here in my hands.

I am profoundly moved that my mother would do this. I feel her fierce will never to forget, and to make what lasts out of something lost.

December 24

I think the hardest moment today was putting the presents under the tree, and knowing that Anna will not be here come morning. What composure we had was swept away: first Beth and myself weeping in our room, the old room I grew up in; and then, thinking we had a hold of ourselves, the whole thing flooding over when I saw the red rimming in my sisters' eyes.

In the end, I am not very good at this manly art of composure; and in the end, I don't really give a damn. How can I not cry when I see in every candle, every light, star, the whole wonder of Anna's eyes?

December 25

It has been easier today, perhaps because of all the excitement. The kids were up, ratcheting around before dawn, and by 7:00 A.M. they were plunging into their stockings, the rest of us watching in my parents' living room. Later we had breakfast and opened the rest of the presents. Each of my sisters gave us a gift "In memory of Anna," and unbeknownst to either of us, Beth and I gave one another almost identical gifts: two brass photo frames for me, and one slightly smaller, older, pewter frame for her. When we get home, we will put a picture of Anna in each of them.

Now it is 3:00 P.M.; everyone else, even my mother, is napping; and I am sitting down in the basement at my father's desk in the corner where he always worked at his business when I was a child. On my right stands an old dust-covered adding machine, with push buttons and a manual crank. A Remington typewriter sits on the file cabinet. Behind me is his workbench, the smell of stiff paintbrushes, and on the shelves above lie neat rows of hand tools, many of them passed along to him when his own father died.

In our basement back home in Hyattsville, I have built a workbench with shelves above, roughly patterned on my father's. He has already given me some of his tools, and when I use them (the Yankee screwdriver, the plane, the hammer) I think of some of our happiest moments: when we made a boat when I was a child, when we'd laugh at "The Honeymooners," and when he sat on a cinderblock in the garage, patiently reading the instructions, as I tried to rebuild my Volkswagen engine.

Now from the bedroom above me, I hear his loud snoring, high-pitched like wind through a screen. He doesn't come down here much anymore. He has sold his business. He lies on his bad back with his pills, the paper, and the remote control for the television set.

I love my father with all my might. And I know that at some time, perhaps now, he must let his life slide through his hands — we must all pass along our tools. But right now I want him to take back his hammer and forge the rest of his days. Right now this letting go, it seems like blasphemy — to let slide the chance Anna fought to have, to let slide what was ripped from her grasp.

December 28
HYATTSVILLE

We are back, and miraculously, there is still snow on the ground. The window boxes are covered. It has been bitterly cold, and at last the leaves are falling from Anna's tree, a few here and there on the crisp snow. They are a color I have never seen before: dark, almost the color of eggplants, but with a brownish cast, as though they have rusted. When you pick them up, they are curled inward, though still leathery, pliable. The nap on the upper sides, like a fine dust, rubs off on the ends of your fingers. At first they don't seem to have any smell. But when you tear them across the veins and breathe them in, they are suddenly alive and musty, like the insides of pumpkins.

Beth's period is four or five days late now, and we are beginning to let ourselves wonder. If nothing happens, she'll have a pregnancy test in the next few days. She has been feeling nauseous, with headaches. She could be pregnant, but then again she has also been attending the Modern Language Association Convention in D.C., the effects of which are probably identical.

December 31

We are heading off to Minnesota on January 3 to be with Beth's family for ten days and to belatedly celebrate Christmas with them.

So we are rushing around, organizing ourselves, seeing friends who are in town for the convention, and still trying to find presents. I feel scattered, diffused, nervous, and a little desperate. Time is short. I can't compose my thoughts. In the last few days, I have felt distant from Anna, as if I have left her behind, or forgotten her — and that scares me.

And there may be something fearful, too, in this passing from one year to another, from a year in which Anna was born, lived, and died, into a year and decade in which she never will physically exist. I don't think I have ever stood on the edge of a new year with such conflicted feelings as these. I want our lives to move on, and yet I would do anything to live her life over. I want to have and love another child without it obscuring or lessening our love for Anna.

Never before have I felt the present so stretched between the past and future, my mind looking forward and back, and the space between seeming to widen. I know we will live the lives ahead of us, and the past, even Anna, will softly recede. I know I can't hold together what must diverge. Yet I can't stop trying either.

Still no period, and Beth's temperature remains slightly elevated. Her period has never been anywhere near this late before, and we are more than quietly hoping now. One of Beth's sentences begins, "Well, and if I *am* pregnant . . ." We calculate that the due date would be sometime in September, when the nights are soft and cool. I catch myself thinking of names, boys' and girls', a brother or sister of Anna's. The thought is happy and sad at the same time. And I wonder what it could mean for a child to be born with the loss of Anna still in the air. Or to grow as a sister or brother of someone who has died before.

January 1, 1990

The new year. And I should state my resolutions:

1. To prepare, prime, and paint the hall, dining room, and living room, replacing moldings where necessary.

2. To build a cedar fence along the east side of our backyard.
3. To keep writing this journal until it runs its course, whatever that might be. To avoid preconceptions, to keep my eyes as wide and open as Anna's. To be unashamed of an honest passion.
4. To remember. To live with loss without forgetting. To hold hard to what I love.

January 2

Very disappointing news today. Still no period, but the pregnancy tests are negative, and our doctor, the same obstetrician who delivered Anna, is referring us to an infertility specialist. We have an appointment for the first of February.

January 3
ST. PAUL

We have just arrived in Minnesota. The land is flat and wide, strewn with lakes and smudged with snow. It is cold. I go out for a jog with a scarf around my face, and later, when it is dark, I hang a pair of skates over my shoulder and, with Beth's brothers, walk down to the small lake behind Beth's parents' house.

On the ice, there is a fire in a barrel and candles flicker in paper bags. We lace up our skates. We race, making figure eights, weaving among the candles. Soon Beth arrives in her knitted hat, boots, and long coat. She stands beside the barrel, hugging herself and warming her hands. The fire glows in her face. She laughs as we wobble and spill. She is beautiful, all alive in the dark, though something here can break your heart. This night. The fire. The sparks that fade, and the swirl of stars.

Where are our children? Where are they hidden in all this openness, this flatness, in the black glare of frozen lakes? What are we skating on? Is it all so empty? Then why this cracking and squalling

85

when I stand on the surface, the teeth of my skates biting in? Why do I feel it heft and sigh? And why, when we walk back to the house — the candles extinguished, the fire out — why do we look back over our shoulders? Why does it feel as if we're walking away?

January 4

It has been six months, exactly, since Anna died, a half turn around the sun.

It was 8:35 A.M. on the Fourth of July, the traffic light, the orange sun hanging in the window of the hospital room. Anna was lying there attached to the machines, so pale and puffy, our arms hooped around her. I had my lips at her left ear, which was swollen up like a funnel, and we were singing to her.

At the instant itself, nothing seemed to happen — I didn't even notice it myself. Nothing changed, no movement, no sound. I felt the nurse's hand like a leaf on my shoulder. She was crying. We were all crying. I looked up and saw the flat line on the monitor. Then I looked for Beth's eyes.

Later, after we had told our parents who were waiting down the hall, we went back in Anna's room. The machines were gone. The tubes and wires were gone. She lay wrapped in a receiving blanket on the crisp white sheets with her music box and a photo of her we had taped a few days before on the crib railing. I picked her up and lay her in Beth's arms. We sat on some chairs in the corner. Beth held her for a while; then I held her; and then Beth held her again. We must have been in there for an hour, with the door closed and the sun coming in. I had never held anything like this before — so still, her lips slightly parted, her skin cold and gray. But it was all right, it was all right. Together we lay her back on the crib.

It was drizzling when we drove home about noon, and I had the windshield wipers on. On our bedroom phone we called our friends and siblings. We went downstairs between bouts of weeping. We must have had lunch at some time and talked with our families — it is all so vague to me now. At dusk, though, I recall the two of us going out the front door and sitting side by side on the porch steps. The rain had stopped. The houses seemed empty, hardly a car on the road. Then came the first faint crackling of fireworks, and the sky flickering beyond the trees. You couldn't see it, but you could imagine: the big sprays of color, red, white, orange, all of it blossoming and raining down.

January 5

Even among our families, the ones we love, we are isolated — and we isolate ourselves — in grief. We are not as spirited. We are not the people that once we were. We walk on our own around the frozen lake. At dinner, conversation touches briefly on Anna, then adroitly it is steered away. We must clear the dishes, get off to a concert, a movie. There are always plans.

At night, Beth is hardest hit by this awkwardness and isolation. We hold each other, and I feel her sobbing. She takes deep breaths, and in the long period between them, she doesn't breathe at all. It frightens me, this; and it reminds me that one of us will eventually lose the other. What will that mean, that kind of aloneness?

But here too, I must steer the conversation and clear the dishes. It is too much to think of. Not here. Not now. Outside the lake is flat and white, the cattails tall and tan in the late afternoon sun. Upstairs I can hear Beth rummaging in the closet, getting her walking boots, hood, mittens — and now that way she tilts her head as she throws her scarf around her.

She calls, "Coming?" and I stop now to put on my things, hurriedly, or else she'll be out the door without me.

January 9

It is 3:30 A.M., and I am up, desperate with this sense that amid all our vacation activities (the visits, concerts, indoor tennis, etc.) I have lost Anna again. People want us to be happy, amused. There are so many things to do and see. And I am a party to all of it. I like nothing better than hiking, a movie, these rousing dinners with all the family, then a few hard sets of tennis to batter myself into tiredness, sleep.

But then I am up like this, in a strange house, frantic to find Anna — or this part of myself that is still her father. I come down here to the basement and sit in front of the sliding glass doors that look out on the darkness. I have brought along a package of photographs, my favorites (Anna over my shoulder, in Beth's arms, and after a bath, hooded and swaddled, her hair plastered to her head — that smell!). I look at them, remembering, and of course I am in tears; though in the end, it makes me feel better, like a reassurance: to touch these things that sting to the core.

January 11

What a fall and winter this has been for wind. Hurricane Hugo. Then that storm we had in December. And now this: a "dust wind" they call it in Minnesota, a warm, moist, steady gale, about fifty miles per hour, that picks up dirt in the Dakotas and carries it hundreds of miles across the prairies, browning the air and the thin layer of snow on the lake outside this window. All last night it was blowing, and this morning's light was dim and diffused, weird, like the light during an eclipse.

When I went out running, I could feel the fine picking dust on my face. It could have been some farmer's topsoil from very far away, and I can almost see him now, standing on a bleak studded field, his coat whipping around him.

I wonder if he misses what the wind has taken? Does he know where it all went? Does he see any rhyme or reason — his scattered hope, this grain of dirt in my eye?

January 12
MIDNIGHT

We have just seen a deer struck and killed on the road tonight. It was about 10:45, an hour ago. Beth and I were driving back here on these windy wooded roads, following Beth's parents in their car about forty yards ahead. We were going thirty-five miles per hour. The road was clear, no ice or snow. We had just come out of a turn and were heading up a slight incline, when I saw them, three deer, all at once in Beth's parents' headlights, like something dropped from the sky.

It was all in an instant. I saw the brake lights glare. I saw the first deer, brown and gray, a whitetail, dart to the left. I lost track of the third. I saw the second one, the smallest, struck in the instant of leaping. I saw it shoot up in the sky, sickly arcing, pinwheeling, its reedy legs clawing the air. I saw it hit down and crumple, and in my own headlights — I pulled up to it and opened the window — I saw it lying there, quivering, eyes so black and wide.

Beth was crying in the passenger seat beside me, crying for me not to look, to drive on. So we left it there, and by the time we had come to the next turn, I too was shuddering with terror. I could hardly drive. It just happens so fast — it is all connected: all the grace in the world so suddenly gone.

No people were hurt in this accident. The car was damaged, dented, bits of brown fur on the grill. Beth's father called the police from home, and when the officer arrived here, clipboard in hand, he said that he had seen the deer on his way over, and it was already dead. It happens all the time on these roads, he went on. They come prancing out of the woods, or they stand stock-still in your headlights. Dumb animals, he said. But not so dumb as horses — "they are like hitting a brick wall." When death comes at them, horses do not budge, even at the moment of impact. But a deer's stillness is released at the end, like some secret energy, or a giant effort. They always spring up with all the life that is in them. It is the last thing they do before they die.

January 15
HYATTSVILLE

Home again. And I realize anew that it is in this place, where a year ago we were waiting for Anna's birth, and where we brought her back from the hospital to live — it is here where I really belong: where there are still unpainted rooms, cracked plaster walls, and where I can feel Anna in my bones once again. It was her presence in this house — and our presence together, the three of us — that makes this place feel as it does. It was on the family room couch where we sat with her, or on these worn front porch steps right outside my window. I can go out and sit there now, my legs together, and practically feel the weight of her head on my knees, the rest of her lankly spread on my thighs, her feet pressed to my stomach. She was exactly that long last spring and summer. My knee to my stomach: twenty-two inches. It is a painful pleasure to feel all this, but a pleasure nonetheless. She would look up at the sky; or when I think of rocking her side-to-side, or grabbing her ankles and bicycling her legs, I hear her giggling and see her smile, her upper lip narrower than the lower.

Sitting in this place, among these familiar things, I know that something here has been truly lived, that my heart is not yet hardened, my soul not dead. This is where she was. This is where we were: in this house, in these rooms, on a street of bungalows and porches, cars in backyards and chain link fences. It is hallowed ground, and I am only partly kidding. Walk these floors and I think you'll know. Look at them closely. Look at everything closely. This is where a life was lived.

January 16

I know of few happier times than the first days after we brought Anna home from the hospital. We showed her off to our friends who visited. I remember she slept a lot then; and when she was awake we'd hold her in our arms, or in the Snugli, or set her, wrapped in receiving blankets, in a blue infant chair that we'd carry from place to place in the house. She didn't cry very often, and for long periods of time, especially in the morning, she seemed happy to sit in that chair and watch us reading, or cooking, or washing dishes. Her presence was altogether novel then, and yet for the most part it felt strangely ordinary, almost routine. We tried to take turns with her. We changed her diapers, and every other day we changed her colostomy bag. As for her nursing, she seemed to be doing well enough; we didn't have to feed her through her stomach tube. She was getting up two or three times in the night, and like any other parents, we were happy but tired, especially Beth. On one of those first nights when she wouldn't settle down, I recall bundling her up in the Snugli, my coat around the two of us, and walking her up and down our neighborhood streets — walking fast, half-proud, half-irked, exhausted — until she fell asleep.

January 17

That more-or-less normal routine, however, was interrupted three days after Anna came home, on the night of February 20, about 11:00 P.M. when Beth had cramps and then sudden and profuse vaginal bleeding, unlike anything we had seen before. It simply sprang out of her, blood all over her nightgown and on the bathroom floor. I got Anna into her bunting and into her car seat. With Beth wrapped in her robe and towels, we drove to the Emergency Room at Georgetown Hospital.

We were there for the rest of the night, first in that large room with white curtains between the gurneys, and then in another examination room with a bed, a fluorescent overhead light, and rose-colored walls. They put Beth on an IV — she was weak, pale; she had lost so much blood — and as they examined her, I sat with Anna in my arms.

Though Beth was in no great danger, I remember feeling unduly scared as she lay there. To lose Beth has been my greatest fear for quite some time, and in my darkest, most secret hours, I have tried to imagine what that would be like. But this was a new and unimaginable fear: to lose the mother of the child that I held in my arms; to think that Anna would grow up without Beth being there. I shudder to think of it now.

January 18

In any event, the bleeding slowed down. Beth was given a drug, Methergine, which would help her uterus contract, and by mid-morning she was feeling well enough for us all to go groggily home.

She spent the rest of that day in our bed upstairs, alternately dozing and nursing Anna, and sometimes both at the same time. By late afternoon, though, and for no apparent reason, the bleeding started suddenly anew, even more uncontrollably now, soaking the bed. I recall one terrible moment in the bathroom. I was on my knees with towels in my hands. Anna was crying; Beth crying, trying frantically to nurse her, and the blood just kept running down the side of the toilet.

I think we were all almost crazy then, and Anna, sensing it, wouldn't nurse. For the second time in less than twenty-four hours we sped to the hospital, Beth sitting on a pile of towels. Dr. Scialli, our ob/gyn, met us in the emergency room. There was another IV and more exams. About 6:00 P.M. he performed the D and C while I stayed with Anna in a long, empty waiting room on the bottom floor, a kind of annex between tall hospital buildings.

I remember it was dusk then, the brown February light in the floor-to-ceiling windows. Anna was mildly interested in the bottle of milk I was encouraging her to drink. I lay her out on the floor to change her diaper. In the window I could see our reflections, and through them I could just make out a twilit courtyard with wooden benches, evergreen shrubs, and flagstone walkways. The moon was coming up, the courtyard empty. I remember a keen urge to take Anna out there in the crisp open air with my coat around her. I remember pushing the doors, but they were locked.

January 19

I couldn't have known it then, but some four months later, I *would* walk in that courtyard with Beth on a hot, sunny mid-morning, on the day before Anna died. On three sides, the courtyard was surrounded by brick medical buildings, and if you counted six floors up on one of them, all the way to the right, you could see the window of Anna's room. On the fourth side, the courtyard was open, except for a low wall that overlooked a playing field, and beyond the trees, the Potomac River, and a wide openness where the big jets were climbing.

Up in the sixth-floor room on that day, Anna lay holding on to her life, with all the machines going, her leg black and mottled. It was five days after her heart surgery, and now the neurologists had been called in to conduct a brain scan. By early that morning, the ECMO machine had removed enough fluid from Anna's tissues so that a doctor could finally open her eyes. I was standing there, looking into her face. It was dawn. I will never forget it. The doctor lifted her swollen left lid and then I opened the right. And there were Anna's eyes, big and dark; they were hers, but they were different now. He shined a flashlight across them and nothing happened. Nothing moved. Her pupils were fixed and dilated. Now I see those beautiful eyes — still those beautiful eyes — but with all of her spark gone out of them.

When Beth awoke from a nap that morning, I told her what I had seen, and later we went out in the courtyard. It was a bright, steaming sun, the sky yellow, and the marigolds were out. We sat on a bench, then walked over to the low wall. We watched the planes ascend, and the college kids, with webbed sticks, playing lacrosse on the field. I remember we were leaning against the wall and holding each other for dear life. I remember the musky smell of Beth's hair in the sun, the glint of the planes, the clench of her fingers, the sky, the window, and the shudder that comes with these acts of love.

January 20

But on that evening in February, as I looked out on the twilit courtyard through the waiting room windows, I couldn't have imagined any of this. I had Anna in my arms, and she was taking little sips from the bottle. Perhaps an hour and a half later, our doctor came down and said that the D and C had gone well. He had discovered and removed a tiny piece of placenta, undetected during the Cesarean, that had lodged in the top of Beth's uterus and had caused all the bleeding. We went up the elevator to Beth's room. She was tired and pale, the IV in her arm, but she was happy to see us. I recall putting Anna back in Beth's arms, and staying there, the three of us, for a couple of hours. The idea was that Beth needed rest, sleep, and a chance to replenish her blood supply. She would stay in the hospital overnight, and I would bring Anna home.

In retrospect — and even with all that has happened since — I have to laugh a little when I think of my first night alone with Anna, though I would have been hard-pressed to find humor in it then. In our lexicon now, it is called "Bill's Night of Living Hell," or "That Cosy Evening," father and daughter: a quiet time to get to know one another.

Everything went wrong. For starters, Anna wailed all the way home — and more fiercely when I slowed down or stopped — so of course I drove like a maniac, keeping my forward motion through stoplights and signs. When I got her inside the house, she was still in full voice; even Jessie was daunted. She spat out the pacifier. I rocked her. I put her over my shoulder and walked her around and around the house. About midnight I got her in the Snugli, and we went out for a brisk stroll. Then, by 2:00 or 3:00 A.M. I persuaded her to at least consider the bottle. It was mother's milk without the mother, and of course she knew it. I was supposed to get fifty milliliters into her, and I recall sitting with her in the living room rocker and calculating that it would be long past dawn before she ever drank that much, even with most of it going down her chin and neck. I burped her. Again I tried to get her to sleep in her crib. As a last resort, I took her into our own bed, and she slept for a couple of hours, while I lay beside her, afraid to move, blitzed with tiredness, and now the feather of light beneath the curtains, and that faint smile on my daughter's lips. She had me wrapped around her finger. She still does.

January 21

Today is Anna's birthday. She would have been one year old. By now she might have been standing, or walking, or crawling up the stairs. I try to think of her first steps, or her first words. I know we would have marked them, just as I mark her absence here. I try to imagine these things, but I don't really see or hear them. It is frustrating, saddening. I can't see her life that might have been. It is all beyond me now.

How will we mark this day? Or should we mark it?

Yesterday we bought a children's picture book (*Where Is Spot?*) and a photo album. This afternoon we will take the book to the hospital and donate it, in Anna's name, to the playroom in the Pediatric Intensive Care Unit. Later, maybe after dinner, we'll go through her photos and begin to arrange them in the album. Then I think we'll light a candle and call it hers. She always liked looking at lighted candles. She would stare in wonder, and while she wouldn't move, you could feel her whole being reaching out toward the flame.

January 22

Sometimes some part of me just doesn't believe she is gone, and I go up the stairs and step into her room with the small rocking chair, the bed, the bureau, and the crib, with all of her things unmoved. Of course she isn't here; nor did I really expect her to be. Still, I push the door closed and sit on the edge of the bed. For some reason I don't touch anything. I am quiet. I know the bureau drawers are stuffed with her clothes and diapers. I see little dresses hanging in the closet, gifts that she was never big enough to wear. It is cloudy outside, and the gray light comes through the dormer windows. I think of pulling the blinds, but I decide not to. The window boxes are empty; the pin oak is bare. I am up in the trees here, up where you can see the roofs of neighbors' houses, shingles and stack pipes, up where Anna spent most of her nights and these early afternoons when she was napping.

In her crib I see the music box, the lamb, and the three pigs that we'd hang over the crib for her to bat at. Now they are still. Nothing moves. The whole house is hushed, and I imagine her sleeping right here, her hair damp, her thumb hanging out of her mouth, her bottom sticking up and her feet scrunched beneath her.

In all of this stillness, I feel as if I am flying apart. I want to stay and I want to leave. I want to be healed, but I tear at the scar. I know she is gone, but I bend over low to hear her breathing.

I wish I could believe that Anna was someplace where she could hear me, where I could speak to her as though over a wall, even though we might not see one another. I'd tell her that we still love her as fiercely as ever, that we will never forget, that the wonder of her only widens with time.

January 25

On the morning after my Night of Living Hell I returned to the hospital with Anna, and I can't think of many other times when I was happier to see Beth. She was still tired, gaunt. She moved very carefully, but she could come home.

For the rest of that day, we tried to relax; I prepared for my Thursday night class, and it seemed we were regaining some composure. Anna was exactly a month old. We had her home. I remember thinking that if we could all live through a month like that, then we could live through just about anything.

There was an incident, though, on the very next day that revealed the tenuousness of all our equilibrium. By any usual measure, it was not a big deal, one of those daily annoyances that occur where people and vehicles are crowded together. Still, I remember it vividly, the sudden wildness of our anger, and the hair prickling on the back of my neck.

It was just before 9:00 A.M. Raining. We had parked in the

hospital lot and were walking across a narrow access road toward the Physicians' Health Building where Anna had an appointment to see Dr. Hoy, her surgeon. The access road runs along a brick wall of the hospital and is used by delivery trucks that take their goods to a loading area between buildings. In any event, we were on the crosswalk. Beth was on my right. I had Anna in my left arm and the umbrella in my other hand. We were proceeding slowly because of Beth's discomfort. We were halfway across and I had just paused to shift Anna under the umbrella, when I heard a truck bearing down from behind us. The driver blew his horn, but didn't slow down until the truck almost hit us. Then the horn blew again, loud and long.

Now in order to get the full flavor of this, you should know that Beth is one of the most levelheaded people I have ever met. She is firm in her convictions, but unlike her husband, she is not usually the sort that flies off the handle in asserting herself. She is friendly, gracious.

So you have to imagine this. As the truck skidded to a stop, its horn blaring, this same woman of quiet dignity turned with a fury, raised her arm, and gave the truck driver the full force of her middle finger.

In an instant, the guy was out of the cab and coming at us, a large black man in a smudgy blue uniform. Then we were all screaming, and with all the moral authority that comes from a child in my arm and my wife beside me, I was going to have it out with this guy who had almost run us down. I shot my umbrella between us like a shield or a sword. It was ridiculous, pathetic, and ugly.

From some deep well of fear, resentment, rage, and—very possibly—racism, this came out of me, shaking and screaming: "You mother fucker!"

And then from probably the same well, the guy, pushing aside the umbrella, and right up in my face: "Who the fuck are you? Fucking fooling around in the road!"

"Nobody's fooling around!"

And Beth, at the top of her lungs: "This is a hospital! There are sick people here!"

And then she was crying. Anna started crying. Beth made it to the wall, her face against the wet brick, sliding down and sobbing.

A security guard ran up. Did we want to file any charges? Call the police?

No. We just wanted to be left alone. We had an appointment. We just wanted to get this poor child in out of the rain.

January 26

December was a record-setting month here for cold, and it looks like January will be just the reverse. It has been strangely warm — twice it almost hit seventy degrees — and the daffodils and tulips, at least a month early, are nosing out of the ground. Why all this weirdness? The hail of acorns last fall? The bitter cold, the windstorms, a hurricane, and now these brave and foolish flowers?

About a third of the fall leaves are still on Anna's tree. They are a pale tan, shriveled, all that deep redness gone. They hang like sad pendants, and I don't know exactly what to make of them anymore. For a long time I have admired their resilience. I still do, though at the moment, I am looking forward to the fresh leaves that will replace them.

You can almost feel them coming now. At the end of each twig there is a half inch of smooth and tender growth, a dark purple; and at the tip itself, hard as a penpoint: a tiny spiked bud.

January 29

I have been doing some building and painting projects around the house of late. From one-by-three inch lumber, and with the help of my table saw downstairs, I made a mock tongue-and-groove door for the storage area beneath the porch out back. Then last week, I painted and assembled the front porch swing that I gave to Beth on her birthday. I like working with wood, the insides of trees. I like to see the grain and all its imperfections. It is perishable stuff, this wood; and so I coat the swing with urethane. But how long will it last in the sun, the wind, and slanting rain? Maybe five years? A decade? Paint chalks and cracks. Wood checks and warps. It weathers and rots.

Yet I know I am most bound, now, to these things that are most imperfect and perishable. We make and love what cannot last. For there is no beauty or poignancy in life everlasting. There is no soul in plastic, no grain, no history, no pitchy vein where life has been. There is no heartwood there, no loss, and no love.

January 31

We did get to our appointment with Dr. Hoy after the incident with the truck driver. He passed some dilators down Anna's throat to make sure it wasn't constricting. He checked her incisions and removed the gastrostomy tube that had been in her stomach since her surgery on the day she was born. He put some gauze and tape over the small hole, and now, except for the narrow scars on the sides of her chest and her colostomy bag hidden beneath her diaper, Anna looked like any normal, healthy child.

Anna would have many doctor's appointments during her life, at least once a week, sometimes twice or three times, for echocardiagrams, EKGs, antibiotic injections, blood tests, or catheterized urine samples. Many of these procedures were painful for her, and before my memory fails me, I'd like to describe my own feelings during these visits.

Like any parents, we were proud to take her anywhere, even to routine appointments. There was always that slightly anxious, but good-natured waiting-room chatter among parents: How old is he or she? What beautiful eyes. And then in the examination room: the familiar nurses who had tiny toy monkeys attached to their stethoscopes, who would tap air from their syringes, or with gloved hands carefully insert the urine catheter.

Usually I would hold Anna during these procedures. It fills me with pain when I remember it. She would scream and writhe, those tears in her eyes. I would hold her tight and talk to her, and Beth would stroke her and talk to her too. Some of these events would take ten or fifteen minutes, and we would press our lips to her forehead, until her pain was over.

Later, by the beginning of April, Anna developed cyanotic spells. Because of her worsening heart condition and inefficient circulation, her skin turned blue when she cried, and appointments like these were more harrowing. During the procedures, we'd sometimes have to give her oxygen. I'd see her face and hands clench, the fear in her eyes, and her lips and tongue going ashy and blue.

When I was holding Anna at these appointments, I felt as though I was holding some interior part of myself. It was so visceral and immediate. When I was in grade school and learning about human anatomy, I had an educational toy, a plastic model called the Visible Man. He wasn't merely visible, but transparent. You could see right through his clear plastic skin to his bones and brightly colored organs. In a larger, life-size version of the Visible Man, which I would later encounter in a biology class, there was a kind of door in his torso, and through it his organs could actually be removed and you could hold the smooth mauve liver and the cranberry-red– and blue-veined heart in your hands, like treasures.

During those harrowing appointments while Anna writhed in pain and her skin turned blue, I was like that Visible Man. My skin felt transparent; a door in my body seemed to have swung wide open, and what I was holding in my hand had come from deep inside me.

We call our children our "flesh and blood," and I used to think it an extravagant metaphor. It *is* a metaphor, especially for men, but now I am not so sure of its extravagance. It seems so literally true. A child born is born from within, and a child who dies is torn from within — a loss in the body, some organ gone, an absence you know from the pain all around it.

February 2

About four or five years ago, I saw a building destroyed, a bungalow, not unlike the one we are living in now. It was an abandoned house in the weedy lot behind the apartment we were renting.

100

A red CONDEMNED poster was nailed on the chained front door. The back door had been broken down, gutters hung off, and in the evenings you could see swallows gliding in and out of the shattered upstairs windows.

One day at noon, some workmen and a bulldozer arrived as I watched from our yard. The workmen stood around, laughing and telling jokes, while the bulldozer rammed a few times at the cinder-block foundation. The house shuddered. The birds shot out of the windows and sat in the neighbors' oaks and on the telephone line. The bulldozer went around to the back of the house and gouged at each corner. It returned to the front, and with its blade up high and skating with sun, it just pushed against the side of the house that would have been the living room wall.

The wall didn't exactly break or cave in. Instead the whole house swayed as one, chimney and all, and as the bulldozer backed quickly away, it simply fell inward, almost gracefully, in a strange slow motion, pouring itself into its own basement.

It took perhaps ten seconds, and that was it. Just a haze of dust, and some scrawny azaleas standing naked in the lot.

Then, about a minute later, something extraordinary happened. As the haze dispersed, the rubble seemed to move, and out from under some beams and chunks of lath and plaster, a pair of small dark hands emerged, dainty and dexterous, pushing aside the debris. It was a raccoon, and it pulled itself free and stood dazed in the sun, its wet nose sniffing. It shook itself. It had those little human hands, black stripes, and a bushy tail. Next it limped slowly toward the road, in no particular hurry. Two workmen moved respectfully out of its way. The rest of them stood and stared. I stood and stared. It was the closest thing I have ever seen to a miracle.

Yesterday we had our appointment with the infertility special-ist at Georgetown. He looked over our records and said we have no time to lose. He took blood from Beth to be tested. Next week I will have another semen analysis, and sometime this month Beth will have exploratory abdominal surgery, a laparoscopy. This is not fun.

February 5

My birthday. The thirty-seventh. And yes, my mind goes back to a year ago on this day when we were able to take Anna out of her isolette and hold her for the first time since her big surgery six days before. Our lives were difficult then, though our arms were full. There was so much concern, and so much joy. I would never have believed that I'd be writing these words. I feared, but never thought, that Anna would die so young. I thought we would all live together. I knew it would be hard, but I thought that a life hard earned would be a life fully lived.

I would never have believed we'd be waiting like this. After all of that. To be waiting and waiting for what has already been.

I wish she were here. I miss her. I wish all of these words were unborn.

February 6

In the next few days (February 23 and 24) after Beth had come home from the hospital and after our incident with the truck driver, some more of our friends came over to our house to see Anna for the first time. Many of these visits are mixed up in my head by now, and yet the feelings and some small incidents have clung powerfully there.

For example, I recall coming down our stairs one morning with Anna in my arms as four of our friends, two couples, were waiting in the living room. Each of the women was pregnant at the time, and all of them had been closely following Anna's progress. During Anna's first month, I had called our friends almost daily from the hospital, mostly for my own sanity, but also because they really wanted to know. Now they were here, and Anna was here.

That moment of putting your child into the arms of another person, a friend or parent, has an almost ritual quality to me now, though at some level I must have been aware of it then. When I think back on Anna's life, I am amazed by the number of people who held her, and by my strange need for her to be held by others.

A few weeks before, when Beth's mother was leaving for Minnesota, I remember insisting on the way to the airport that we stop at the hospital so she could hold Anna again. Now I felt that same thing as I came down the stairs with our friends waiting in the living room. I needed them to hold her. Not just to accept her, but to feel all of the life inside of her, and all of her fragility. I think they did that. And I think I had this odd sense that if enough people could really hold her and know her, then somehow that would help her get better, like some kind of laying on of hands.

Some of my best memories of Anna are seeing her in the arms of others, either sleeping, or fussing, or smiling and bug-eyed. The things that people would say or do. My father cradling her tight to his chest with his thin arms shaking. Or my mother holding her right up to her face, nose to nose, eye to eye, unblinking. And our friends. One of them rocked her, another smelled her hair; another sat with her for a long time in our dining room, silent and staring, as if to take all of her in. Our friends who were pregnant held her close to their own unborn children. I will never forget that. Those children, two boys, were born in the months and weeks before Anna died. I recall holding each of them for the first time. One was as light as Anna; the other big and chunky, a smile that wrapped around the sides of his face. We still see these children when we see our friends. We touch them and hold them. I guess I don't believe it anymore, but I still wish this holding could help them live.

February 7

On the night of February 25, four days after Beth returned from the hospital after her D and C, we had to return to the emergency room, this time for Anna's sake. It was difficult. Usually she was happy, but now she was cranky, pale; she had a fever; and she would barely nurse. I remember Beth calling the pediatrician and weeping on the phone. Anna had been home for a week, and three of those nights Beth had spent at the hospital. It was all too much. Our doctor said to bring her in; he would call the Emergency Room and make the arrangements. So again we drove those familiar roads in the dead of night, and a half hour later Anna, this tiny child, lay on the big gurney between the sliding curtains. They took blood and urine. They put her on an IV. At one point Beth had to leave and I was on the verge of passing out — it is so hard to get a needle into the vein of an infant. Anna cried so hard that we gave her oxygen. I remember holding the end of the plastic tube in the little valley right under her nose. Breathe, Anna, breathe. It's all right. Easy. I was saying it as much to myself as to her.

February 8

Where does a person's strength come from? When I think back on those times, those full nights in the emergency room, or those days around Anna's death, I am amazed by what we did. Sadly, I already feel somewhat distant from the person I was then. I'm not sure that I could do it all now, again. So where did the strength come from at the time?

First, I should say that, so far as I can tell, it did not come from any religious faith or down from the skies in the form of divine intervention. More likely, it had its root in that godforsaken stubbornness, that digging in of the heels, that for better and worse is at the heart of me. But there was so much more.

I think that in large measure the strength that we had came from the people around us. The efforts of doctors and nurses. Our families. The look in a friend's eye. Or for me: to see Beth leaning over Anna on the other side of the gurney, after a Cesarean, that bleeding, a D and C, and those sleepless nights. How could I do anything less than all that I possibly could?

And then — and perhaps most important — there was the strength that came from Anna herself. That is the real difference between the person I was then and the one I am now. I believe there can be a kind of courage even in people so young. Anna was so small, and sometimes her pain so large. Anyone who had held her as she lay on that gurney or as she lay dying — anyone who had felt her fighting so hard — would have been fierce with all of their strength.

February 9

For the next week, February 25 through March 4, it was Beth's strength that carried us through. Anna had a severe urinary tract infection. She would stay in the hospital on IV antibiotics until her urine was sterile, and Beth, who was not about to stop nursing her then, would stay there with her.

It was a long week, especially for Beth. In the mornings I'd work here at home, and in the afternoons go to the hospital with clean clothes and other comforts for Beth. As I came in the door I'd often see the two of them in the navy blue Naugahyde chair by the window. The IV pole stood on its wheels beside them, the bag hanging with clear liquid, the pump clicking, and the plastic tube disappearing beneath the receiving blankets that swaddled Anna. She would be nursing. I'd see her face in profile, pressed to Beth's breast, her small rounded nose, high forehead, sweaty with concentration, oblivious to the man at the door.

Perhaps, as I remember this, I feel a tinge of jealousy, though mostly there is admiration. At the moment I came in, Beth's eyes might have been on Anna, and then they would have looked up at me. They have a soft and smoky quality when she is tired. Her hair is dark with that swatch of gray in the front. When she nursed Anna there was often pain, yet there was peace as well. All this I would see in her face — and so much more that these words can hardly touch: that fullness or completion, a giving over of herself, like water smooth down a spillway.

Last night, soon after we shut off our lights, Beth started to cry, sobbing. This still happens to both of us. She said she was thinking about holding Anna when Anna was dead. As I recall, Beth held her in exactly the same way as when Anna was alive, or as when I walked in that other hospital room on those afternoons months before and saw the two of them, nursing. On that day Anna died, Beth had her in the crook of her left arm, up snug to her chest, with her right hand smoothing and smoothing Anna's hair.

February 10

Today a colleague of Beth's, a friend of ours, mentioned that when he sees Beth at school, she often seems to be hugging herself, her arms crossed tightly in front of her. I haven't really noticed this before, though when I think of it — or when I think of her — I realize he is right. Many mornings when I come downstairs, I find Beth beside the stove with her arms around herself — those same arms that held Anna — just as our friend has described. Usually she is wearing her terry cloth robe, and looking vacantly out the window while she waits for her coffee water to boil.

During Anna's last days, Beth and I, already thin, lost ten or fifteen pounds, and neither of us has gained it back. All the fullness of nursing has gone from Beth's body, all the serenity gone from her eyes. Like those figures of Modigliani's, we are hollowed and elongated. Beth's neck is narrow; you can see the bones that come to a V at the top button of her nightgown. There is a sinewy beauty about her now, for so much has been stripped away. As I see her standing at the stove, hugging her long arms, she seems to be holding all that is gone and all that remains. She is holding herself together.

Now I feel the effort of this, the dignity of this: to compose herself for the day. She pours water through the grounds, checks the clock, and holding the steaming mug in both hands, she goes upstairs to dress for school.

February 11

When a person you love dies or is suspended in grave danger, the world, especially in retrospect, seems filled with signs or clues. I don't believe that the world or some all-knowing power actively gives us signs. Rather, I think that in circumstances like this, when you want so desperately to know what will happen, you begin to see and read the world differently. With something so central so fragilely suspended, everything matters, everything means, anything at all could tip the balance. So apparently unrelated events seem imbued with significance, or predictive, even causal, qualities.

On that birthday of Beth's (December 16, 1988), when she was seven and a half months pregnant with Anna, and on that same day that she had the sonogram that showed some fetal anomalies (that strange cystic structure) — on that day I gave Beth a bouquet of three roses. About a week later, Beth hung the roses, heads down, to dry on a hook in our pantry. We forgot all about them until one evening last summer, long after Anna was born, when it was clear that her heart surgery was imminent. Beth went into the pantry and found that one of the roses had fallen off the hook. I remember she looked scared when she came into the kitchen with the small shriveled rose in the palm of her hand. She said it felt like a premonition, and I remember trying to brush that notion aside. It was ridiculous. Pure superstition. But then something made me get a needle from Beth's sewing box downstairs. I took all three of the roses, and pushing the needle through their tough short stems, I pinned them together, stem to stem, and hung them back on the hook.

They are hanging there now, the three roses, like shriveled bells. In the afternoons, the winter sun washes across them. They are weightless, parched and preserved. The stems are hard, rosewood. This spidery husk was once a bud. And the flower itself: so red-black, crisp, a papery sound in the web of your palm, a faint scent at the pointed heart.

February 14
VALENTINE'S DAY

8:00 A.M.: I am writing this in the hospital cafeteria where I have come for a bagel and orange juice after seeing Beth, in a pale blue hospital gown, off to her laparoscopy/hysteroscopy. She will be under general anesthesia during the procedure, which should last for an hour or so. I should be able to see her again by 10:00 or 10:30 A.M.

I have been somewhat scared in the last few days, thinking about this moment: seeing Beth walk down a hall where I am not allowed to go. A laparoscopy is a straightforward exploratory procedure, "same day surgery" with "minimal risks." I should be able to bring her home this afternoon. Still, I'm afraid I can't help thinking about Anna, about holding her as they shot in the anesthetic, and sensing some danger, while knowing that the mortality rate for her heart surgery was only 5 percent. The chances were with us. There was little reason to expect her to die. She had been through her most dangerous days.

But then there were "complications." I suppose there can always be complications. So yes, I am anxious, probably more than I need to be.

These things I run into. On the way over here to the cafeteria, I passed Conference Room A, where more than a year ago we attended our birth classes each Wednesday night, where we would practice breathing techniques, and I, at one point, would nearly faint — I had to leave the room, careening out the door — as our instructor described an episiotomy, the "E-word" Beth and I call it now.

Then, down another hall, in a part of the hospital I don't know, I passed a closed door with the sign "Autopsy, Histology." I actually paused there, and it crossed my mind that I could knock on the door, go in, and ask the doctors if they remembered seeing a five-month-old baby girl who passed through here.

"Passed through." Those are the words I would have used, as if she had been here visiting, a child lost and wandering. I might have talked to the person who wrote the autopsy report. Do you remember that hair? You wrote, "Scalp hair is brown." But off the record, what else did you notice? What more did you feel? Was there any sense of the life that flew out of her? Any sense of what she meant?

So much of my life, it seems, has been left here in this hospital — or so much of what feels so central. This is a place of painful memories, a place of sickness, but also a place of so much care. I feel oddly comfortable among these doctors and medical students chatting over coffee at the tables around me, with their white coats, pens in pockets, and ID badges. It was like this quite often when Anna was here: this anxious waiting while some procedure was under way. A bagel, the banter of voices, time to kill. And all this anticipation to see a familiar face once again.

9:20 A.M.: I am back in the Family Waiting Room for Same Day Surgery. There are magazines, toys (a dollhouse that opens in the middle), and on a desk a phone that rings when a patient is out of the recovery room and family members are allowed to visit.

On the way back here from the cafeteria — it's not exactly "on the way" — I went up to the maternity floor, through the swinging doors, and down the short hall to the Intensive Care Nursery. Inside, I could see the familiar fluorescent lights, parents bent over isolettes, and hear that hum of activity. None of the nurses who were closest to Anna was on duty. But one who was coming in the door, who was never Anna's particular nurse — I don't even recall her face — she looked at me, stopped, and said after thinking for a moment, "It was Anna. Right?"

I wonder how many other parents haunt these halls, with their eyes filled with the lives of their dead children. The nurses must see them coming, drawn and wandering, lost in these bright halls of their dreams.

How could this have been? Just a year ago. It was in that room, in one of those isolettes, beside that window, and beneath those shivering blue fluorescent lights. I belonged there then. I could put my hands though the portals and touch her skin. It all seems so unbelievable now.

10:10 A.M.: Our surgeon has just come to the door, and we talked in the hall. He said that Beth was all right, groggy and recovering. She'll be in a haze for a while, but I should be able to see her in an hour.

As for the exploratory surgery, they found some things. Beth's left fallopian tube is functioning but was damaged by the uterine infection (remember all the blood, that piece of placenta) she had a month after Anna's birth. Moreover, her right tube had been altogether closed over with scar tissue, thus severely reducing her chances to get pregnant in the last six months. During the procedure, however, our doctor was able to reopen the tube, and with periodic X rays (hystero-salpingograms) in the next few months he can determine whether it remains open.

So. I am trying to take this all in. It strikes me as very hopeful. There is apparently an explanation for our troubles, a problem that has, at least for the time being, been corrected. Our chances should be better now. I want to tell that to Beth.

The phone rings.

About noon: I am in here with Beth in this little cubicle with a curtain across the front. She was awake for a while, but lies asleep now beneath sheets and blankets on a small bed that can be converted into an easy chair. She has her knees to her chest beneath the covers. The IV is dripping. The nurses say she will fade in and out of consciousness as the anesthetic wears off. So I hold her hand, and I can feel it go slack as she falls away.

When she was awake I gave her sips of water through a straw. I told her what the doctor had said.

"Do you want to have twins?" she said groggily. She has been on a respirator, a tube in her throat, and her voice was only a whisper. I saw the waves of pain gather along her eyebrows. Cramps. She squeezed my hand, and it all reminded me of her labor with Anna. Not so intense, but the way she exhaled, making a little O of her mouth. The pain passed; another sip; and her eyes rolled up and closed.

The next time, as her eyes flickered open, Beth said, "My throat." Then, "It must have been so hard for her," meaning Anna, who was so long on the respirator, who is so deep in the marrow of both of us. Beth was thinking of her, even as she slept. And I am thinking of her too as I sit here wide awake.

How I have come to know this feeling of waiting beside a bed. It has a strange fulfillment, just the being here, though for long times nothing is said or done. I see Beth's hair fanned back against the pillow. It is darker than Anna's, less wild. She has this dignity, even under sedation. I watch the blankets lift and fall, lift and fall. Nothing to me now is more moving than this.

February 18

Beth is mending, slowly. Two days in bed with Jessie curled on the blankets beside her, *Practical Homeowner* magazines, and a book on Yeats called *The Vast Design*. Now she sleeps on the family room couch after a morning walk around the neighborhood.

A week ago I was describing some events that might be interpreted as signs or premonitions. In my present state of mind, I can say categorically that I don't believe in such things — there is no supernatural agency — though I also know that there were times, when we were pushed to the wall, that we became more open-minded about these matters. We engaged in something like superstition ourselves. Once was on the night of June 29, the day after Anna's heart surgery. The surgery itself had been successful, but it was clear by now that something was going terribly wrong. Anna's blood tests showed signs of acidosis. She wasn't urinating, her kidneys seemed to have shut down, and fluid was leaking through all her capillaries and into her body tissues (edema). That evening, the doctors gave her a drug called Bumex, a powerful diuretic that, we hoped, would start her urinating again. I remember Dr. Kim massaging her swollen lower abdomen, and then a few drops of liquid came through the catheter and into a plastic cup. The doctors and nurses were actually cheering. We were beside ourselves. If Anna could continue to urinate, she would probably live. She could expel the excess fluid. She just had to keep peeing.

Later we went outside for a walk, dazed with exhaustion and excitement. It was around midnight, muggy, the thick cones of light hanging beneath the street lamps, and the sidewalks slick with mist. We walked out on Reservoir Road beside the low magnolias, went east toward Wisconsin Avenue, with the whole hospital humming behind us.

And then, with that weird humor that comes sometimes amid great seriousness, it struck me that if we took a right on Thirty-fifth and went down a few blocks, we'd hit P Street; and since peeing was the name of the game, we damn well ought to be walking there. So we must have gone five or six blocks along the rumpled brick sidewalks of P Street, up one side and back on the other, striding fast and determined, before returning to the hospital. There was something ridiculous, self-conscious, and comical in all of this — this odd dance to the gods of urine — and yet at the time it felt as though we were onto something. This might be one of those strange constellations of events and thought that was meant to be. As we strode down P Street, Anna would be urinating, recovering. I know it sounds ludicrous, but a part of me could make out the pattern, a little corner of the vast design in which she was surely meant to live.

Soon after we returned to her room, though, we could see with our own eyes that she had stopped urinating again. The catheter was empty. The cup didn't fill. Her tissues swelled; the respirator chugged; and her eyelids bloated shut.

If there were signs, then I had misread them. And if there was some vast design, some determining pattern or power, then it would exact more hardship and pain. It would allow our child to die.

Several years ago, long before we ever tried to conceive, I published a story about a family with a newborn baby girl. The story is told by the husband, in retrospect. He recalls a cold Saturday morning when his wife was off at a puppet show with their older daughter, and he bundled the baby in the car and drove to the pharmacy for a newspaper. He was only in there for a couple of minutes — he got the paper and chatted with the pharmacist. But when he returned to the car, the child had died; she was the color of porcelain as she lay in her basket on the passenger seat.

I will let you make of this what you will. Since Anna's death, I have been unable to read this story, though I know it by heart. It makes me wonder and it makes me sad. The story goes on after the death of the child. The husband tells how his wife and he were blown apart, and how they made pained and tentative gestures to come back together.

Someday I hope to read it again, though I am not anxious to do so now. I suspect I will be disappointed or embarrassed, for I am not the person I was when I wrote it. I am more like the husband who tells that story, more like a character whose real life is the fiction.

February 20

The unseasonably warm weather continues. The forsythia blooms. Through my side window, around which I built these bookcases, I can see the arching yellow spires and star-shaped flowers against the fence between our neighbor's yard and ours.

As for Anna's tree, it seems to be in a dormant period, conserving itself while the other trees in the neighborhood are pushing their buds. We may soon have blossoms along our street, even as Anna's tree holds on to those same dozen or so leaves from last year.

For months there have been no other leaves on any other trees. The evening sky is lacy with bare twigs and branches — except for this. Perhaps Anna's tree is out of sync, its inner clock gone wild or asleep. Or perhaps this is still some fierce tenacity, some holding on long after the time for letting go.

Is the tree alive? I think so. The twigs are pliable, the tips wine-red. But what saddens me now is that if this tree is to live, the old leaves must be replaced. What is clenched so fiercely is forced away.

Still, the heartwood stays. And so the branches. The same roots cling to the soil. Invisible fibrils. Capillaries. In these finest filaments: the greatest transformations, the place of passage. Solid into liquid. Liquid into gas. Arteries become veins. Bodies into souls.

None of this is replaced. None of this is lost, or forgotten, raked into sheets and left on the curb.

I wish I could live in these places of passage. I wish I could know how she went. A whole life passed through a membrane. In the smallest vessel. In the thinnest root hair. I still need to know how it happened for her.

Februrary 21

By March 4, almost a year ago now, the course of IV antibiotics had brought Anna's urinary tract infection under control. She was taken off the IV, and on that day I brought her and Beth home from the hospital. They had been in there together for exactly a week.

As I glance over the rest of that month on our last year's calendar, I am struck by how normal it all was, how filled with those little delights and surprises of having a new child. After the craziness of January and February, we seemed to be settling into something like the lives we had envisioned for ourselves — only it was better, in fact, than we could have imagined. Of course we were aware of, and frightened by, the hurdles to come. We knew that Anna's heart would eventually need to be mended and the lower end of her genitourinary-digestive tracts would have to be straightened out.

But these forsythia outside my window, and these daffodils, tulips, and lilies, already a half foot out of the ground — they remind me of the promise of those days last March, the feel of sun on my back and dirt on my hands on any number of those cool late-afternoons. I was crazy about gardening then. I bought books and pamphlets. When I finished at the typewriter, I went out and tilled and re-edged the flower beds. Sometimes I would bring Anna out there, bundled in the stroller, or sometimes I would look up toward the back porch and see Beth holding her, tight to her chest, framed in the doorway beneath the metal overhang.

What I am trying to describe is just the feeling of Anna being around, and the sense that she was not immediately threatened, that our lives together were becoming routine. On Tuesdays we took her to the hospital to see her cardiologists; on Wednesdays she saw her pediatricians. On Thursday nights I taught my class, and on the weekends we often had visitors, friends or family, and we began taking Anna out to other people's houses as well.

Still, the best of it was that sense of the three of us, like a slow warmth, the going through each day and night without any emergencies. I ache now for the simple routine of those days, monotonous perhaps as the clicking arc of the windup swing. That sound was like that of a great clock, filling the house with predictability. You could follow that sound, and Anna would be there. You could go out for a walk, or a run, you could teach a class, putter in the yard, and when you went back in, you could go in the family room and see her swinging, or climb the narrow stairs, go quietly into her room, and by the light of the streetlamp shimmering through the pin oak, or by the sweet and cloying smell, or by the rhythm of her breath or just the hush of your own, you would know that she was there. You could be sure.

February 22

What gets lost in the litany of medical facts and events is the character of a child like this, that sheer happiness and wonder that flies in the face of what, to adults, is often so worrisome. Except for when they directly caused her pain, Anna couldn't have cared less about all the IVs, the scars, the colostomy bag, even the tube that had been in her stomach.

None of it seemed to matter to her; it was no big deal; and something of this attitude carried over to us. Recalling it now, I am struck by how the supposedly abnormal can be so readily incorporated into the normal rhythms of a normal day. I think of changing her colostomy bag, an olfactory nightmare: me peeling off the old pouch, trying not to gag, handing it to Beth to dispose of, and Beth preparing the new one (cutting the hole in the bag and adhesive wafer) while I cleaned the remaining adhesive from around the stoma, sopped up the fresh emissions, then lined up the stoma and the hole, and pressed on the new bag. All of this happened in a couple of minutes, a flurry of activity, like those wild pit stops you see in car races, Anna screaming all the while. It was not pleasant. And especially later as she began having blue (cyanotic) spells when she cried, these periods could be alarming.

Yet in a matter of minutes after they were over, she would be beaming, kicking her legs, staring at the bright dancing horses over her crib. It was nothing. What were we worrying about? That plastic bag sticking out from the left side of her diaper with the end folded over, pleated, and cinched with a rubber band — in a short time we hardly noticed it. It really *was* no big deal.

February 23

I am getting ahead of myself again, but a month later, in April, we would have Anna on IV antibiotics at home for nearly two weeks because of another urinary tract infection. A nurse showed us how to do it. Then three times each day (morning, noon, and evening) Beth and I would wash our hands, assemble sterilized needles, plungers, and prefilled syringes. We hung the medication bag on the IV pole, spiked the bag with the end of the IV tubing, squeezed the drip chamber, and for a moment opened the roller clamp, allowing the narrow tubing to fill. Then one of us put a needle, still in its plastic sheath, on the end of the tubing. With Beth holding Anna and sometimes nursing her in the small rocking chair in the corner of Anna's room, I would squat down, hold Anna's left leg, and with an antiseptic swab clean the injection cap of the catheter (or heparin lock) that went into a vein in her foot. Then I would take the sheath off the needle of the saline syringe, insert the needle into the injection cap, and slowly push the plunger, flushing the catheter, while feeling with my other hand for Anna's response. Often it was painful for her, and I would slow down or wait until the pain abated. Next I would remove the needle of the saline syringe, insert the needle of the IV tubing, tape it, reopen the roller clamp, adjust it, and begin the infusion.

Why do I tell you all of these details, every step of changing a colostomy bag and starting an IV? In part it is because of this incessant need to vindicate myself, to say over and over that Anna didn't die from any want of love or care.

But there is something else that I want this to show, a simple and obvious point, though one I must work to remember: there are capacities we have that only our children can unlock, these parts of ourselves that we do not know. When I feel my life constricting, when I sense in this quiet house the loss of possibility and personal strength, I must remember what it was that we were able to do. I must remember who it was that we still might become.

February 26

I have days when I feel nothing, and days when I feel like this, when I speak Anna's name in this quiet house, when I stand in her doorway and try to listen.

If she could hear me, I would tell her this: There are evenings when your mother sits in the corner of the family room couch, with her shoes off and the lamp beside her. I come in the room and sometimes as I turn toward her, my eyes do not fall first on her eyes, but on the place on her shoulder where your head would rest.

That soft knoll at the base of her neck. With your eyes closed and nose burrowed in. I know it well. We have shared that place, and for the same reason, as deer who lay in the same bent grass.

Now as I settle on the couch, I see your mother's sad eyes, and I return to that place all brimmed with your absence. Sweat and spittle, soured milk. We know you still in the palms of our hands, in the curves of our shoulders, in these shallow basins we cannot fill.

February 27

You almost knew it would come. A bitter cold snap. First wind, up to forty miles per hour. Then three nights in a row with the temperatures below ten degrees. And this morning a flurry of snow, the forsythia brown, the lilies limp and ragged on the ground. In the newspaper they are saying that the cherry blossoms are in danger, nipped in the bud, frozen at the very moment of opening.

During her heart surgery, Anna too was chilled, her body temperature lowered dramatically so that all of her functions would slow down while she was maintained on a heart-lung machine. I have always had difficulty in thinking of this, this period of coldness as the doctors bent over her opened heart. It flies against all of my instincts to hold her tight and warm, to get from her bureau the booties and bunting, and the white cap my mother made.

That's how we had her dressed when we took her out on those cool nights last March, sometimes for a walk beneath the trees on our street. The blossoms were out, the buds bursting with scent. And that chill in the air? I didn't fear it then. We thought we could hold her warm and alive, safe in her pod, all packed in the Snugli, her head on my chest and my coat around her.

February 28

Perhaps because of this weather, and perhaps because of Anna's death, this morning I am remembering that day four years ago when I was out on Shelf Moor on the Pennine Way. It was the fourth of January, 1986. We were on an exchange program, living for a year in Sheffield, England. Beth's family was visiting, and on that afternoon, I was hiking with her brother, Fritz, in the Peak District, that remote moorland between Sheffield and Manchester.

It was cold, the sky low and gray, about three or four inches of snow on the ground. We parked the car on the side of the narrow road and climbed over the stile, following the vague trail. We walked for a couple of miles straight out into the gray-white moors with the gray-white sky clamped upon us. A sharp, picking wind blew from the west. Now and then we would stop and look around, getting our bearings with our map and compass. It was all open, barren, white, and vast; everything to see and nothing to see, the snow whipping through tufts of heather and crackling grass. We went on, each rise like a series of shelves, one leading to another.

At one point, and from out of nowhere, a big jet glided by to the west, circling for Manchester airport. It was so low and close that we could see the oval windows and the bright red letters on the tail: British Airways. But it hardly made a sound, as if it was coasting, its roar all sucked up in the wind.

Again we went on, climbing gradually, and as we approached what seemed like the edge of the land, we saw a small pyramid of stones to the north, and we left the trail to see it. It began to snow. Out here the moors were more rugged, austere, like pictures I've seen of the moon. We went through gulches, filled to our hips with snow. The ground immediately underfoot was frozen, crusty, but lower down, you could feel the bogs, a slight quivering and hollowness, dark and peaty, like a thought at the back of your mind.

The pile of stones was a cairn, a simple landmark, with a metal disk on the top and the elevation, two thousand feet, engraved on the disk. Nothing more. The wind had worn the stones smooth and round. They were glazed with ice, and on them the blown snow had left delicate whorls, like something incised, like fingerprints.

We spotted another cairn, apparently on the brow of the last rise, and we headed toward it, wading through the wiry heather. The snow came hard and oblique. We were about a third of the way there, climbing on a low ridge, when I saw in the distance what seemed at first like some craggy rocks, randomly scattered or protruding from a wide shallow bowl in the earth. Coming toward it, we could see dark edges, angles, sharp and gnarled things in all this white smoothness. Some old farm equipment, I thought, abandoned machines. But why so strewn? And way out here on the moors where there were no farms for miles?

Making our way down into the shallow bowl, about two hundred yards wide, we found great ragged hunks of metal, shorn and twisted aluminum, wheels, engines, cylinders, rusted rods, and here almost an entire wing, dug into earth, clawing the air, the snow ticking its skin.

On one of the engines, on a metal strap beside the toothed flywheel, there was a handprinted sign, no larger than a business card:

> IN MEMORY
> TO THIRTEEN AMERICAN
> AIRMEN KILLED AT
> THIS SITE 3-11-48
> R.I.P.

March 2

For a number of weeks, I was intrigued and strangely moved by what I had seen. I don't think of myself as the kind of person who wanders around old battlefields. Nor, as I have mentioned before, am I particularly religious or spiritual. Yet I still remember a kind of holiness about that white and lonely place, with the snow and the wind and the mad scattering of what had once cohered. Such devastation. And the airmen. I imagined a plane twirling out of the sky, and the frozen instant when they must have known. Kids from Kansas, Georgia, Jersey. Hayseeds and shortstops sunk like plummets in the black peat. I saw their silent fires burning in the fog.

Is all of this agony so vain?

Now I think of those airmen in this crazed connectedness of all of our perishing. The squeeze of Anna's hand as the blipping line went flat. Or the squeeze of my own and Beth's, cold and sweating across the armrest, as we glide toward the runway, toward earth, home, and the still moment of touching down.

On the next day I went to the Sheffield library and, on microfilm, looked up the *Sheffield Telegraph* for November 4, 1948. It was right there on the front page, along with the headline announcing that in America Truman had just defeated Dewey. I copied it down in my notebook.

Thirteen American airmen are believed to have died when a B 29 Superfortress crashed on Shelf Moor in the Peak District yesterday evening.

The plane was found by two members of RAF Mountain Rescue Squad, but mist and darkness prevented rescuers from getting the bodies over the wild, inaccessible moorland.

The search was called off until daybreak today. For 2 hours [the rescue teams] struggled across the moors from Snake Pass, and after covering acres of isolated moorland, the last dying embers of the Superfortress were discovered.

Though they were able to establish that 7 bodies of the crew were in the wreckage, they were unable to trace six others. The wreckage was scattered over an area nearly half-a-mile.

"As soon as we reached the spot, it was obvious that no member of the crew had survived," a leading member of one party said. The spot where the aircraft crashed is one of the most dreaded on the moorland. Only three years ago a Lancaster bomber crashed in almost the exact spot with heavy loss of life.

"The tracks along which the bodies will be brought will be the same as those along which we brought the Lancaster crew," he added.

March 4

Today it is eight months since Anna's death, two-thirds of a year. And this afternoon as I glance over the lines I copied here two days ago, I am stopped by those words spoken by the member of the rescue party so many years ago: the bodies of the American crewmen would be carried along the same tracks as the bodies from an earlier crash.

Why does this strike me so? — as if there is some order in all this dying. The same tracks. A shared path — probably exactly the same path that we walked, Beth's brother and I, on that cold January day exactly three and a half years before Anna's death. The bodies of the airmen must have been canvas-covered and strapped on litters that tilted wildly as burly men, one on each end, lugged them over the gray moors. I see them now, seven in a row, bobbing like dinghies. And what of the other six? "Unable to trace." Burned to ashes.

Untracked. Unable to be carried over the worn path, their cinders, like flung seeds, lost in all that whiteness. What of them?

On the sixth of July last year, two days after Anna's death, and the day following the autopsy, we drove downtown to Lee's Funeral Home to identify her body before she was cremated. The funeral home was a high-ceilinged Victorian building with wide mahogany moldings, darkly festooned. In a parlor with leather chairs and a glass-top desk, we signed some papers and wrote out a check. The funeral director led us to an old elevator in the hall. Anna was in there, he said. I remember it was an Otis elevator — it said "Otis" on the steel tread on the floor. I remember, too, that the man had to push open two elevator doors: the first mahogany with a small glass window reinforced with wire mesh, and then a sliding crisscross metal gate that clattered to the side.

The man switched on a light, and Anna was in there, wrapped in the pink receiving blanket, her tiny swaddled body strapped on a full-length stretcher. Her face was exposed, and it was hers. I told the man — I remember his name now; it was French, like mine: Lo Bélanger — I told him that yes, that was her. That was nobody else. I remember looking at her for a short while with Beth right beside me. She was still so beautiful, even then, with her eyes closed and wisps of hair along her forehead. I remember turning to leave, stopping, and turning back and bending toward her. I remember Beth saying no — and she was right. We were all beyond the point of touching. She was out of our hands, gone; though I still hear the clatter and snap of the metal gate, and see her strapped on that canvas litter, like those airmen wavering across the boggy moors. Along the same tracks. Along the same path where we will walk, or be carried, again.

Anna's body was cremated on the following day, like the bodies of the six airmen who could not be traced, their ashes strewn on the brow of Shelf Moor. We have thought of scattering Anna's ashes somewhere, but we cannot think of a place, if there is one at all. So we will leave them for the time being in the small blue box on top of my bureau. I open the box now and then. I unzip the Ziploc plastic bag inside and touch her ashes with the ends of my fingers. They are not horrible. For the most part, they are fine, soft, and powdery. They stick in the whorls of your fingers, except for some small white shards of shattered bone, like shattered shells. They have no smell, no taste. I make a small pyramid in my palm, in the heart of my palm. I hold her there. I feel her there. And I know what it is that is absolute.

March 5

We have recently learned that a colleague of Beth's, a friend of ours — not a particularly close friend, but a friend nonetheless — has colon cancer. The tumor is large and may have metastasized. The prognosis is cloudy, and probably not good. He will be operated on this Wednesday.

Two nights ago, Beth talked with him on the phone, and we are moved to tears by what he says: He is doing very well. He will maintain a positive outlook. He will live with relish what remains of his life.

It seems that for him, there is a kind of peace that comes after great turmoil and outrage. He spoke of going to the hospital chapel after a CAT scan, and having "what I can only describe as a religious experience." He felt a vast peacefulness, he said, a giving over of himself "to a higher power."

I am happy for this. And in a strange way, I almost envy it, a period of real transcendence, or acceptance, a profound tranquillity. Perhaps this only comes to certain kinds of people, or perhaps only to people whose lives are directly and immediately threatened. As for me, there are only these vague hintings, strewn debris on a snow-covered moor. And even there, there is no tranquillity, no acceptance. The wind speaks of the airmen's agony. These ashes cry of a terrible absence.

Rather than peace, what I feel is more like an intense concentration of self, a steeling of the will — almost against the will — and not a giving over of anything. When I think of our friend's condition, I am filled anew with this familiar sadness and aimless fury at all that is random, devastating, and unjust. Our friend and his wife are the parents of three adopted children. They are good, caring people. So why must they suffer? Why must the children suffer? How can there be peace when there is so much unsolved in my heart?

March 8

During that relatively calm month of March last year (before the at-home IV antibiotics and blue spells of April), we were probably like any other parents with their first child at home. What extraordinary attention we gave to the little things Anna did. Those first smiles and cooing sounds. Or the way she began to wildly kick her legs when she was happy and lying on her back.

I was particularly taken by the way she would stare at certain things. There were (and still are) the bright horses that circle above her crib, and the bears that dance over the changing table in the bathroom upstairs. But what most enthralled her, at least inside our house, was the small chandelier, an old tarnished one from my parents' home, that hangs over our dining room table.

I think I was holding Anna when she first discovered it. I had just brought her downstairs one evening and I was carrying her through the dining room toward the kitchen, when I felt her eyes lock onto something and her head turning hard to keep it in view. I stopped, and she gazed transfixed at the chandelier. She clutched her hands beneath her chin, her mouth still and open. You would have thought she had seen Christ ascendant in those five tapered bulbs of light, each surrounded by a glass globe and supported on a curving narrow stem of brass.

From the time I was three, when my parents built their house, until I went away to college some fifteen years later, I lived with that chandelier. It was at the center of the house, in the dining room, where my family ate all of our dinners, where I kicked at my sisters' shins beneath the cherrywood table, argued with my parents, made up, and where afterward I would often do my homework, books and maps strewn on the table, the scent of Lemon Pledge, as my father read the *Courier News* or watched "The Honeymooners" in the living room, and my mother, at the kitchen sink, sang like Edith Piaf.

I have lived a lot in the light of that chandelier, which hangs now in the center of our own house where I can see it through the hallway as I work here at my desk. In all those years in my parents' house, however, I don't think I ever really *saw* it. The chandelier was just one of those things, like the wallpaper, or the school-day sandwiches that appeared on the counter, or the neat row of plates gleaming each morning in the dish rack.

Perhaps for people like me, it takes having a child — or even losing one — to see, as if for the first time, the simple things that connect our different lives. If Anna had lived, she too would have eaten her dinners beneath that chandelier, and we would have laughed, argued, done our damage and made our amends, all in its silent ministry of light.

March 11

Last night, about midnight, as we were reading in bed, I heard it through our open window, that distant plaintive honking, faint and forlorn, oboelike: *woo-hoo, woo-hoo*. It came five or six times, like something shooting across your mind, fading fast, and it was gone.

Then early this morning, a Sunday morning, while I was out for a jog, I heard it again. I was running up Farragut Street between the old frame houses, and as I heard it I saw an old man on his front walk looking up at the sky behind me. He called urgently into his house, and an old woman, presumably his wife, appeared on the porch in curlers and a pink housecoat.

"Look!" he said to her. "Look!"

He was pointing up there, so I stopped running and turned around, looking up.

And there they were, a huge ribboned V across the gray sky. Way up. Maybe forty or fifty, all white, their wings going, their necks straight out like compass needles, and all the time that faraway sound, thin but piercing, a sound with weight in it, pain and sorrow, like a sound a human could make.

"Geese," I said. I was standing now on the man's sidewalk. We were all looking up, perhaps in the same way that Anna always looked up at that chandelier or at the trees out behind our house.

"No," the man said to me. The skin on his face was tough and wrinkled. He wore a brown cap, and he seemed to know what he was talking about. "They're trumpeter swans," he went on. "See the necks, how long. They're from the Eastern Shore, heading north. I hunt a lot down there. Ducks, geese. But you don't touch the swans, not them." He shook his head. "God, just look at them!"

For a time we stood without talking as the long wavering line moved like a dream or a vague aspiration. I have seen many kinds of birds in flight, but nothing quite like this. Those white wings so wide and calmly moving. And yet the sound — it seemed to have nothing to do with the wings, as if it came from beyond the wings, or lower down, so close that in your own throat you could feel it.

March 12

When I got home from running, I went straight to our *Field Guide to the Birds*. The old man was right. The long necks and white plumage gave them away. They were trumpeter swans, also called whistling swans. They winter in the bays and estuaries along the Maryland and Carolina coastlines, and about this time of year they begin their migration, thousands of miles, to breed in the tundra north and west of Hudson Bay. With the first burst of spring — as though restless already with the prospect of comfort — they yearn for the barren slopes.

But what does this have to do with Anna?

I'd like to see her death as a kind of migration, a passage from one place to another, and for a purpose, like feeding or breeding. I'd like to think that. And somehow these swans *do* remind me of her: their sound, their white necks moving slowly across the morning sky. But as I think of them, I cannot help but knowing that in the fall they will return with their young, circling high, then skidding down into Chesapeake Bay. And my daughter will not be with them.

There is probably nothing I can know that is *like* Anna's death. No journey, no migration, no metaphor will do. Still I keep thinking of those trumpeter swans and all their beauty, their extended wings — even as I stare out my window, and see above the blossoming trees this pure and empty sky.

March 13

We have just gotten some disturbing news about our friend who was operated on for colon cancer. The surgery was successful, but the cancer had already spread to his lymphatic system. Of twelve places that were tested, the cancer was present in ten. We do not know the prognosis, but I am filled with sympathy for him and his family, and once again I feel this aimless fury.

For the past three successive Saturday mornings, we have been going to a series of classes on adoption. The various adoption processes are labyrinthine, as is the question, for us, as to whether and when we should actively look for a child. For the moment at least, we have decided to delay the start of any adoption process for about six months, during which time (beginning next month), Beth will be on a heavy-duty fertility drug, Pergonal. If we don't conceive our own child by next fall — and even perhaps if we do — then I think we will get the adoption ball rolling. One way or the other, we want to be parents again.

At various times during these adoption classes, there are guest speakers: lawyers, social workers, representatives of adoption agencies, or adoptive parents. It was late during the second class in that stuffy church basement with about fifty of us listening to a presentation, when the next guests, two adoptive parents, came in the side door with their three-year-old daughter, who had been born in India. The girl was small, her brown legs spindly. She wore a blue smocked dress and a blue bow in her black hair. Her eyes were very dark, and when she walked, she almost pranced, looking cautiously at all the strange faces. Then, holding out her skirt, and aware of the favorable attention she had attracted, she pranced anew.

I can only describe what I felt then as a pang of recognition. It had most to do with the girl's willowy body, her long narrow limbs, and a certain fragile, impish quality in her carriage. This is awkward to explain, but it felt almost as if my own body had known the body of that girl in the way that I had known Anna. You simply don't forget these things; they are in your bones: the way a leg tapers, or the toes curl. It seemed for a moment that in this girl's presence, I was so near to it all again.

I remember feeling Beth's hand on mine beneath the table where we were sitting. She was feeling all of this too, and probably more powerfully than me. I think I now have a sense of what it means when people say that their heart goes out to someone, like our stricken friend and his family, or this little girl from Delhi. Something in your body seems to actually reach out, tendriled and groping; or it even takes wing, like that ribbon of swans heading north and home.

March 14

Over the last three days there has been a record heat wave, and I've been scraping, sanding, priming, and painting the front porch railing and balusters of a friend's house. These are the friends who, just a year ago, gave us that dogwood that later would die, the first of Anna's trees.

That was on the evening of March 25 last year. Our friends and their two young sons had been passing around the flu for a month, so this was the first time they were all able to meet Anna. They invited us over for dinner. I packed the Swyngomatic and diaper bag in the back of the car. As I recall, it was raining or drizzling, and we carried Anna across our friends' lawn, one of us holding the umbrella. When we got to their porch, we saw the dogwood, its roots in a black plastic container, standing beside the railing where I have been painting for the last few days. It was about chest high, gracefully shaped, and tied on the end of each of its branches was a pink ribbon, the narrow ribbed kind that curls when you run it along the sharp edge of a scissors. There must have been thirty or forty of them, and when we planted the tree in our backyard a few weeks later, we didn't remove the ribbons. Instead, the sparrows picked them off, one at a time; and even as late as last fall when I was raking up acorns and leaves — long after that dogwood had died and Anna had died — I'd find those frayed lengths of pink ribbon here and there in the bushes or woven into the nests that the sparrows had made in our garage or in the rafters of our back porch.

March 15

Now, as I write this, the sparrows are nesting again. You can hear them shouting outside my window. Or if you stand still by our back door or sit in Beth's study, you can watch them copulating, the male fluttering on the back of the female, and then both of them gathering strands of grass, some mossy stuff, and bits of Kleenex, all of it packed in that same niche in the rafters where they had hatched their young last summer.

I never saw them, the young, leaving the nest last year — it must have happened while we were with Anna at the hospital, during her last days. But I will always remember that week beforehand, when we knew she was about to have her surgery, when I was working in Beth's study, and in the mornings, Anna would be rocking in the swing beside the desk, and through the window I'd watch the adult sparrows arriving with food, and the young ones hinging themselves open, that small red arrow in the heart of their throats.

March 16

I've been thinking, with a chill, of Frost's poem "The Hill Wife," which begins,

One ought not to have to care
   So much as you and I
Care when the birds come round the house
   To seem to say good-by;

Or care so much when they come back
   With whatever it is they sing;
The truth being we are as much
   Too glad for the one thing

As we are too sad for the other here —
   With birds that fill their breasts
But with each other and themselves
   And their built or driven nests.

The poem is about the quiet desperation of the hill wife whose house is empty of children. There is only her laboring husband, and he is clearly not enough. One day, with nothing to do in the house, the hill wife follows her husband out to the fields where he plows and fells trees. She sings to herself and rests on a log.

And once she went to break a bough
   Of black alder.
She strayed so far she scarcely heard
   When he called her —

And didn't answer — didn't speak —
   Or return.

She simply wanders away in her own misery, and her husband never finds her.

I worry about this — the wandering away — especially at these times of the month, when we study Beth's temperature chart like hieroglyphics, a whole scroll of charts, month after month, year after year, the long zigzag of temperature, like a slow unfurling, stopped but twice. Once for a child I cannot name. And once for Anna who lived and died.

130

I see in these charts the cryptic lines and circled days when we have laid ourselves out as if in prayer, and nothing has come and filled our lives. I am afraid of these empty houses and oft-furrowed fields, their quiet pain, and the row after row of nothing.

March 19

When I awoke in the middle of last night, I found that the bed was empty beside me and the pillows were gone. The house was dark and quiet. I got up, pushed open Anna's door, and there on the bed in the pale light of the streetlamp was Beth, sleeping beneath the covers, her head turned away from the crib toward the wall.

I simply didn't know what to say or do. I didn't wake her. I got back in our own bed, but there was no way that I could sleep. So again I got up, looked into Anna's room, and heard Beth's slow and even breath. Then I came quietly downstairs, put on my sweats, and went out for a run in the cool night air.

March 20

I have mentioned this before, that strange feeling when you run by your own house in the dead of night, and see it as if it was someone else's: the cars parked on the concrete driveway, the porch swing hanging still, the empty white flower boxes, and dark windows, one of them partway open on the front dormer.

What kinds of lives are lived in there, beyond the scraggly yews, the porch, and asbestos shingles? What I felt as I jogged by our house that night was a twinge of distance, as if I was only imaginatively connected to the web of concerns within its walls. I didn't live there. I didn't know the people. I could run by that house as I had run by all the others. I could see it from outside, perhaps as the hill wife had seen the farmhouse from across the fields, even as she wandered away.

But where do you go when you stop looking back? What does it mean to never return? I hadn't even reached the end of the block and turned up Thirty-ninth when my mind flew back inside our house, into the dormered room with the crib and the rocker, where my wife slept in the poster bed without our child in her arms.

When I returned, I went up to Anna's room and Beth was still asleep, unaware of my travels. I stood in the doorway and remembered how I had stood there a year ago and heard their breathing, Beth's and Anna's, filling that room with a gauzy comfort. I went back into our own bedroom, undressed, and immediately fell asleep. When I next awoke, there was light in our curtains, the whir of traffic, and Beth was lying, sound asleep, beneath the covers beside me.

I suppose we both have our small and separate wanderings and, I trust, our separate returns. There is so much we know of each other, and yet so much that we cannot know, even of ourselves and these dark corners of sadness. But one thing I do know — and if we are to live and not resign: we must always come back to this trouble of love, to these small rooms of our greatest difficulty.

March 21

I cannot put Frost back on the shelf without saying something about "Home Burial," that poem about a husband and wife who are each locked in their separate grief after the death of their infant son. I have just reread it, and I am shuddering with its pain and power. How I feel for that woman who has seen her husband digging the grave, the gravel leaping up, and then leaning his spade against the wall — at a time like that, he spoke only of birch fences. And how I feel, too, for the husband who, however awkwardly, now yearns to share in his wife's feelings, yearns to "speak of his own child that's dead" without provoking her resentment. "Don't — don't go," he says,

> *Don't carry it to someone else this time.*
> *Tell me about it if it's something human.*
> *Let me into your grief.*

132

But they are so hardened to one another. There is no letting in, or letting go. The poem ends with them raging, the wife opening the door to leave, and the husband screaming that he'll force her to return.

What do I make of something like this? Except to say that it scares me, because it feels so terribly true and perilously close — this damage that grief can do.

If a child dies, then we must surely speak it; and if it is human, then we must tell, and each of us must listen. It is horrible enough to have lost this much. It is almost unthinkable to lose any more.

March 22

This morning while making our bed, I remembered how we used to prop Anna up against the pillows, sitting her there like a little queen, where she could watch us puttering around the room, getting dressed in the mornings. We have a picture of her sitting this way last March. It is such a typical look for her: eyes all agog, staring straight at the camera, her hair mashed against the pillow, and her hands held up close to her chin and shoulders.

Her hands were still fisted then, but not in the way that a fighter clenches his hands. Rather, she held her thumbs beneath her curled fingers, as if to hide or protect them, in the way that she held them when she was born.

Now I go through all of her photos and look at her hands, their slow uncurling and the emergence of her long thumbs. What a thing to see and remember. At first we had to pry them open to clean out the grunge that stuck in the creases there. By March, though, we could fit little toys in her hands. In April she began to bat at things suspended above her, and in May she would bring her hands together around her toys and hold them on her own. By the time she went in for her heart surgery, of course, her hands were as open as yours and mine, though she tended to sleep with them loosely closed, with one of her thumbs at the edge of her lips.

When I think of her hands, I can smell her palms and see those long tapered thumbs, almost as long as her forefingers. I have no idea where they came from. Neither Beth nor myself have unusual hands. When I look at my own, they seem blunt and gnarled, graceless, the nails bitten, the squat thumbs, all paint-flecked, and veins tunneling beneath the skin.

How did her hands spring from ours? Where did they come from, and where have they gone? I search my palms and I haven't an answer, though this is the place where I knew her best. I still feel what it was to scoop her off that pillowed bed: left hand beneath her head and neck, and right beneath her bottom; then lifting and pulling her close. These hands know that. This is where I live. In these groping things, hammer–hit and mashed in the jigsaw. They are like a fighter's hands, you well might think.

But I am well beyond the point of fighting. And yet I am beyond the point of giving in, or giving up. Or ever letting my daughter go.

Anna died with her hands clenched, and our index fingers wrapped in her palms. In a way, she died with us in *her* hands. And when we slid out our fingers, her hands didn't move. They stayed like that, tight and curled, like delicate shells, her long thumbs locked over her fingers.

March 24

Snow this morning, wet and heavy, bending down the azaleas that are just beginning to bloom. Yesterday, though, it was warm and breezy, and we took the day off to drive down to Charlottesville to see Jefferson's Monticello. The site is spectacular, on a gentle mountain-top overlooking the foothills of the Blue Ridge. In the woods, the feathery redbuds were out, and tulips filled the gardens. I was struck by the simplicity of the house, how it opened to the outdoors, all those windows and skylights, as if you were out in the wind and sun, even when you were inside.

It must have been the quality of the air — the hyacinths, the first sweet day of spring — that made me keep thinking of Anna. Last year that day came on March 26 when we took her to a wedding at an old gristmill not far from here. On that day, like this, the oaks and elms were budding, the tulips out. Anna was in her pink dress and white sweater. With all the people around — her first big public outing — she was quiet and watchful. I remember that Beth and I took turns with her, and some of our friends held her too. The breeze came through the wide gristmill windows, smelling of blossoms; and once during the reception, I recall seeing Beth far across the room, alone with Anna, nursing her at a corner table.

Perhaps because of the different setting and my distant vantage point, I saw them for a moment (or at least now, as I reconstruct it) in a way that I didn't usually see them at home. *What* I saw was no different: the way Beth held Anna across her lap, or the way Anna would rhythmically open and close her hands as she nursed, and periodically would stop and look up at Beth. Still, it seemed as if the strangeness of the setting, or its public nature, brought the intimacy of their gestures into greater relief. This was my wife and daughter, but for a moment it felt as if I was seeing a painting or an etching, some small domestic scene, across a loud and crowded gallery. I was part of the crowd. I felt my distance. And then I felt that surge of pride and intimacy, and a little relief, as I went over and pulled up a chair beside them.

How these moments come back to me, even as we stood yesterday in a group of tourists, in the wash of light at Monticello. Jefferson and his wife had six children, two of whom survived. And in the graveyard down the hill you can see through the iron fence some small stone markers that are too distant to read.

Should we have left some marker for Anna? Some small thing cut in stone? Some plot of earth to keep her bones? Here? Or here? This ground to touch, these words to stay, this grass to keep? A place?

I don't know. For *every* place seems to speak of her. Our small yard beneath these oaks; or an ocean away, the wind-worn moors. On Jefferson's own grave there stands an obelisk that doesn't even mention that he was president. It says that he was the first governor of Virginia,

that he wrote the Declaration of Independence, and died in 1826 —
on the Fourth of July.

March 26

By yesterday morning the snow was gone, and I spent the afternoon seeding the bare spots in the backyard, and then fertilizing the entire lawn. With one of those three-pronged cultivators, I scratched and loosened the soil, then laid in the seed, letting it slide through my fingers. Next I covered the area with a layer of straw and watered it with a fine mist. Now I wait.

It is not without pain that I do this seeding, but it is also with such a belligerent hope. Nothing new can replace what was loved and gone, though something new can also be loved. I hold these seeds as I have held those ashes. A small pyramid, weightless, gone with the slightest breath. I hold them and I know what it is that fights and lives, and what it is that fights and dies.

Not ten feet away stands Anna's tree. On all the twigs and branches, the pointed ends have opened, and slender tongues of green growth are sliding into the light. Amazingly, there are still four dried leaves from last year, hanging on as for dear life, hanging from the same pointed buds where the new growth comes.

March 27

I hope this dogwood continues to live, and I hope this grass seed grows. For it has all been getting more difficult of late, especially for Beth. Neither of us knows exactly why — how can anybody know these things? In part it may have to do with the probable beginning of this Pergonal treatment, which, for all intents and purposes, is our last chance to have a child of our own. Moreover, there is just something in the air with the coming of spring: these same smells and blossoms as a year ago, and the sparrows nesting in the porch rafters.

In the last few weeks, I have seen a distance in Beth's eyes that scares me. And last night at a friend's house, she wondered aloud if her life was worth living.

A day doesn't go by when we don't talk about Anna, or don't try to talk about what we are feeling. But I am getting the sense, perhaps belatedly, that all our sharing may not be enough, that what Beth needs I cannot wholly provide.

In so many ways she is the stronger of us, though I am usually the most willful. When the fall semester began, just two months after Anna's death, Beth plunged into her teaching and committee work. And I, teaching just once a week, plunged mostly into this. It is possible that at first this was hardest for me: each day the house so quiet, and all the remembering and putting down. It is still painful, though probably not as painful as the distance Beth increasingly feels between her work (professing) and the focus of her real concerns (Anna, our family). In addition, the sympathy and support of some of her colleagues has diminished faster than her need for it. They have turned their minds back to the living — it is only natural — while we must still live by remembering.

March 28

Sometimes I think that Beth should be writing this. She knew Anna better. She could tell you more, and more accurately. For after all, it was she who kept this "Baby's Calendar" that I so depend on to re-create Anna's life. And it was she who took most of these photographs that I pore over each day. She was the chronicler during Anna's life, and I mostly came to it after her death.

I feel unsettled about this, though I don't know what else to do. There is no way, Beth has said, that she would spend her mornings writing something like this, though she is glad I am doing it. Over these months, she has seen a few of these pages. She says it is weird to read about herself almost as a character in a story; and as I am writing this, I feel the same way: a certain squeamishness, or claustrophobia.

I don't like my heart this close to the words. I don't like all this sorrow. Nor do I like the uncertainty of the characters' fate, especially when the characters are ourselves.

If there was another voice I could use, or another story that was more compelling to me now, then surely I would write it. But this is what presses. This is what I feel and know. It is often painful, yet there is also a satisfaction in filling a page, getting it down — this is what happened and this is how we live. For me there is nothing more urgent to tell.

March 29

It is not getting any easier for Beth. Yesterday was a bad day at school: her proposals were voted down at a department meeting, and she just hasn't the stomach, especially now, for the snakepit of academic politics. When she shut off her bedside lamp last night, she just cried and cried. And then, after she got up for a Kleenex, I heard her go into Anna's room.

When I got up and stood in Anna's doorway, Beth was sitting in the dark, going back and forth in the rocker, her face in her hands. She had one of Anna's blankets over her shoulders, like a shawl, in just the way that she would have had it there when she was nursing Anna. I asked her if I could come in, and she nodded yes. I sat on the bed with the spooled crib between us. Though I frequently go up there in the mornings, and perhaps Beth visits Anna's room in the afternoons while I am out painting, this was the first time we had been in there, together like this, since the first months after Anna died.

Beth just rocked, and I just sat there. The same pale light of the streetlamp came through the budding pin oak, the bare limbs shadowed on the walls. Anna's dresses hung in the open closet. The mirror was above the bureau, the plastic horses dangling over the crib. It was after midnight, and a few cars passed on the road, but all you could really hear was the creak of the rocker, and another sound, thin and rhythmic, that you were only imagining.

For a half hour we stayed like that, until Beth got up, came over, and sat beside me on the edge of the bed, her body still slowly rocking. We touched hands and held them there. Then with the blanket still over her shoulders, we went back into our own bedroom.

March 30

Beth has had another dream about Anna. This one not a dream where she searched and couldn't find her, but one where she was pushing Anna in the stroller, a sort of comfortable dream of everyday life back when Anna was alive. In the dream, Beth said she could touch Anna's face and hair. It was definitely her, except that her eyes were the wrong color, a bright blue that was puzzling, though it didn't make the dream unpleasant.

I wish I could dream of Anna, and perhaps all this wakeful thinking of her has somehow precluded my dreams, or used them all up. If I had it in my power, I'd like to dream something like Beth has dreamed. Something ordinary and tactile. I would be holding Anna again on the swing in the backyard. It would be early in June. Twilight. Fireflies in the grass. I would feel it in her body when she looked up at the trees, and I would feel all of her fragility and all of her strength. I'd be afraid for her, but mostly I would be hopeful.

In this dream I'd like to dream the wakeful dreams that I was dreaming then: about the time after Anna's heart would be mended, and we would have her home again, out of danger. I had fantasies about reading to her and dispensing great wisdom, or one day playing tennis, or even teaching her to throw a curveball, holding it with the seams and snapping her wrist like Whitey Ford. She would have probably been bored by, or rejected, all of this, though it hardly seemed to matter. It was the free range of my wakeful dreaming that perhaps most distinguished the person I was then from the one I am now. Now I don't *have* those dreams so much as I re-create them. When an only child dies, not only is the child unimaginably gone, but gone too is so much of your imagined future, a bright window bricked and mortared.

April 1

April. Last year this was the month when Anna's life, and ours, became a little more complicated, when she began having those blue spells, and when it became increasingly clear that her heart would need mending sooner rather than later. This April, too, promises to be complicated, though in a very different way. Beth's period began this weekend — another disappointment — and on Tuesday morning at 8:00 A.M., we will be back at the hospital where she is to begin the Pergonal regime: first a baseline ultrasound and blood test, and then I am to give her the first daily injection of the drug, to be continued at home until she is ready to ovulate about the middle of the month.

In the meantime, we are trying to maintain some sense of humor about all of this. Mostly it will be a pain in the ass, I have heard Beth saying to a friend on the phone. And sometimes we have visions of white-jacketed technicians reading lab results and saying, "Now! In the next hour!" and we will race home, march upstairs where the bed will be open, the dog locked out, and I'll have a split of wine on my bureau, two glasses, a candle, and matches, everything ready to go. There has got to be some niche of pleasure, even in all of this.

April 2

Two nights ago, we heard a concert by the Tallis Scholars, a Renaissance vocal ensemble. They sing a cappella in the manner of English boys' choirs, except that the sopranos here are women. I have heard such choral music before (at evensong, in England), but I have never been so moved. It had little to do, I think, with the words, which were all in Latin anyway. Rather, it had to do with the way that I was hearing the music now: the purity of these voices, the harmonies so ethereal, so fragile, and yet so palpably filling the air.

There are certain sounds that seem to speak to me of Anna, as though her presence is carried somehow on the quivering air. I know it is all in my mind, this presence, but it doesn't altogether feel that way. For a time, it feels as if something is really there — something different than a memory — as when you sense without seeing that someone is at your door.

April 3

Yes, the Pergonal therapy has begun. Giving an injection, like getting one, is mostly a matter of holding steady and holding back the fear of pain: the giving of it rather than the receiving. Like most things for me, it is more daunting to think about than to actually do. The idea of all those needles in Anna's veins was somehow more frightening to me than holding her and seeing them sliding in. So, too, with this.

The process, though, touches on something that we have been feeling since Anna's death. For much of my life, I have had this sense that my skin is a kind of boundary between myself and the world, a place where I could stand guard and regulate traffic. When a child dies, however, it is as if all of your pores are thrown wide open, your thick skin so suddenly pervious.

In the epigraph to his poem "Heart's Needle," W. D. Snodgrass cites these lines from an old Irish story, "The Frenzy of Suibne":

"Your daughter is dead," said Loingsechan.
"And an only daughter is the needle of the heart," said Suibne.

The needle of the heart. That is it exactly. Our skin is unblemished, no blood, no scars. Yet through these merest pinholes come deepest piercings, and drop by drop the deepest pain and deepest love.

An only daughter is the needle of the heart. That is you, Anna. That is always you.

141

April 4

On this day, Anna has been dead for precisely nine months — another period of gestation, or just the beginning of an ongoing gestation that will last as long as our lives. I suppose that what I am feeling now is different in some ways from what I was feeling nine months ago. The pure shock has worn away, and some of the anger expended. The pain is still there. The needle strikes just as deeply, though with a little less frequency, and a little more surprise.

What I mostly feel is a bittersweet yearning, like these tulips out my window that bend toward the morning sun. When I sit down at this keyboard and look at the calendar and all these photos, I am not usually crying anymore, though I can still feel her in my palms and along the insides of my arms. And now, this second, it is almost as if I am holding her again. I am standing and rocking her slightly. I am looking for that bluish tinge along the edge of her lips while she is crying and looking at me with that wide-open look that means that she is scared and doesn't understand what is happening.

I was holding her like this just a year ago today, in the cardiologists' office while Dr. Shapiro and his assistant did an echocardiogram, an ultrasound of her heart. While I held her, the assistant slid the lubricated transducer around on her chest, and you could see on a screen an image of Anna's heart and watch it pumping like a fast-clenching fist. As with other images of the insides of her, I was transfixed by what I saw. I remember it now: not so much the shape of her heart, but the motion of it, the wild kick of it, like a cat in a bag.

If I ever become a religious man and I am in need of some icon, totem, some image to live by, I think it would be my daughter's wild little heart, and its vital thrust despite its defects. Of course I have seen those artists' renditions of Christ's heart, the "sacred heart," with the spokes of light all around it. That image moves millions, but it doesn't move me. That heart is so idealized, so static, more of an emblem than the thing itself. I can't in my own heart feel its pulsing. And it is the pulsing — the urgency of that — that makes all the difference.

142

April 5

Moreover, as the doctor slid the transducer on Anna's chest that day, he turned a dial below the screen, and the room filled with the *sound* of Anna's heart: a huge, swaying, swooshing sound, with peaks and valleys, like the sound we heard that night last fall, in our tent on Piseco Lake, with the wind all around, the trees rocking, and the wild waves lashing the shore.

The doctors looked at the screen and listened to the sound, and I held Anna tightly. I have come to recognize that quiet and sober concentration in a doctor's face, the way he purses his lips when he is seeing something he'd rather not, when he is formulating news that will be unwelcome. Two other cardiologists came in and studied the screen. They pointed to shapes that I couldn't understand until they explained. They showed us the hole between her ventricles (VSD) where blood leaked through, and also the smaller hole between her atria (ASD). It was the narrowing of her pulmonary artery (pulmonary stenosis), though, that most concerned them. It seemed to have gotten worse, constricting more rapidly than they had hoped. Anna's heart was working harder to pump less blood through the narrowed artery and out into the rest of her body. Hence those tinges of blue around her nose and lips, the beginnings of cyanosis, an insufficient oxygenation of her blood, especially when she was excited.

As yet her condition was far from critical, though this did mean that her heart would have to be monitored even more closely, and the timing of her corrective surgery (ideally at one year old) would have to be moved up to sometime, probably, that summer.

In the meantime, we were to watch for Anna's blue spells, and bring her into the hospital if they got suddenly worse. A cardiac catheterization (an exploratory surgery where dye is injected into the heart) was scheduled for April 12, a week later.

April 6

Beth's parents are visiting us for a week, and while they have been making phone calls downstairs, I have come up here into Anna's

143

room with the keyboard, my calendar, pictures, and notes. I am sitting on the rocking chair, with the crib to my left, the three dormer windows to my right, and the poster bed straight ahead of me. The door is shut and it is almost quiet — just the ticking of Anna's clock, and from beyond the windows, the splash of tires through puddles on the road. Out there it is cold and drizzly — we could have snow tonight — while in this room, among all her things, I feel safe and warm and sad. For here, over the edge of the crib, hangs the blanket that Beth had over her shoulders some nights ago, the same blanket that we would double over Anna on cool days like this. And here on the flannel sheet lies one of her shirts with the three snaps at the bottom, and here is one of her bibs, unwashed, with tan and pinkish stains.

I bring the shirt to my nose, but I can't smell anything. I touch the end of my tongue to each of the stains and taste the faint sweet strawberry flavor, the taste of her antibiotics, and the dried remains of her saliva itself.

Is this sick or maudlin? If I was reading this at some earlier time of my life, I would have suspected it was.

But I tell you now that when a child dies, this is how you live. You pay attention to what is lost, relive the love and life, and relive the death. You do not turn away and are not ashamed. For when there are no answers, you can only live and you can only feel. And if you can, you live it all, and feel it all — touch and taste, shed every tear.

You must not let the world rip you out of your heart. You must love the dead as you love the living. For what you love is all that matters, and what you love is all that lasts.

You must not let the world rip you out of your heart. It is the only thing that you have.

April 10

The Pergonal is working. Over last weekend — each morning we spent at the hospital — we saw on ultrasound five eggs developing,

144

two in the right ovary and three in the left. One of them was mature enough for fertilization, and on Sunday night I gave Beth the injection of HCG (human chorionic gonadotropin, a hormone), which should have released the eggs by this morning.

All of this is hopeful, and even now as I am writing, there are sperm swimming their dark channels and eggs springing, like flowers, from follicles.

About a half hour ago, I was washing my hands in the upstairs bathroom when I saw Beth through the window, sitting out on the swing in the corner of the backyard. She is still sitting there now in her white turtleneck, pink cable-knit sweater, sneakers, and gray sweatpants. She had a book in one hand, but she wasn't reading; she had her coffee cup on her lap, and she was just staring at it.

I went downstairs, out the back door, and sat on the swing beside her. Her hair has gotten longer of late, and it brushes the top of her narrow shoulders. She said she was thinking of Anna, but that is all she wanted to say. I got up and walked around the yard where our bedsheets flapped on the clothesline. It is a beautiful spring day, azaleas glaring in the sun. Anna's tree is sprouting the smallest of leaves, and the oaks are furry now with tiny male flowers, borne on dangling yellow catkins.

Yet even today, in all this fecundity, our fiercest hopes are tinged with sadness. There is snow on these blossoms. There is pain even in our mergings. For we plant these seeds in the same scarred ground where Anna has lived and left her mark.

What could it mean to be pregnant again — after what has been conceived and never born, and what has been born and died? I sat again on the swing, though we didn't say anything. I knew there was something human to tell, and yet sometimes it all seems beyond all words, just as so much seems so beyond us now, so out of our hands.

I went back in the house, climbed the stairs, and found myself watching Beth again from the bathroom window. She sat there like that, small and fragile, with her knees together and her coffee cup still in her lap. I saw her close her eyes and drift into sleep; and she has been sleeping there for a while now — I have just looked again. Her book lies closed on the bench beside her. Long strands of her hair move in the breeze. How I wish there was something that I could do, something that was certain and something that mattered. If I could put Anna back in Beth's arms. If only I could awaken her to that.

April 11

This morning Beth cut some red and yellow tulips and arranged them in a vase on our blue-checked tablecloth right below the chandelier. Last year, about this time, she did the same. My mother's birthday is April 9, and because we couldn't travel too far from the hospital, my parents visited us again that weekend. I remember Anna rocking in her Swyngomatic in the dining room doorway as we ate Cornish game hens for my mother's birthday dinner. On the side table against the wall behind my usual seat, Beth had put two lighted candles, and between them the vase of tulips.

At some point just after we had begun, Anna must have become restless in the swing, because I have a photo here of her propped up on my left shoulder as I was trying, with one hand, to work my way through the hen. In the photo we are both in profile, our heads side by side, facing opposite directions, me looking straight ahead, and Anna looking behind me. You can see her ragged hair hanging over her collar, her narrow arms draped over my back, and her tiny nose — so much smaller, thank God, than mine.

But what interests me most here is something that I can clearly see now, though I must have been oblivious to it at the time. As I was engaged in the conversation before me, Anna was engaged in her own private pleasure. In the photo, she is staring over my shoulder straight at the candles and the bunch of tulips. Her eyes are huge, and her face is filled with delight. As I look at this now, it makes me wonder just how much of her life I must have missed — she looking one way and I the other. How many secret pains or pleasures? What did she feel as she lay alone in her crib, wide awake as the morning sun came through her dormer windows? Or what did she feel as she lay in the same sun, a few months later, as it rose over the quiet city, beyond her hospital window, and washed her face with orange?

So much of this writing is all periphery. I describe her hair, eyes, nose; I measure her feet and fingers. I run around and around the perimeter, but I can never really get inside. I cannot hold the flame. I cannot hold her life as she lived it. I see only these flickerings.

April 12

We are doing our 1989 income tax return, and this, with a pang, we fill in on the first page of the 1040 form:

Exemptions
6a X Yourself
 b X Spouse
 c Dependents:

Name	Check if under age 2	Relationship	No. of months lived in your home in 1989
Anna Loizeaux	X	child	5½

How do I describe the power of such simple information? Yes, we had one dependent. Her name was Anna Loizeaux. She was under age two. She was our child. She lived for five and a half months in our home.

When I write her name, I am flooded with tears, and it is hard to explain. For somehow it is as if she is inside of that name. That is her. That is who she was. That name could have been no one else's.

But what troubles me now is how a name can exist and a person can't, how two things so fused can be rent apart, one alive and the other dead. In my mind they are one and the same. The name and the person. I write her name and she should be alive. I write it over and over — and still she isn't alive. That just doesn't make sense. I just don't understand.

"What will you call her?" the nurse had asked, as she held her, still gleaming, so that Beth could touch her.

"Anna," I said.

And I remember saying it over and over, backward and forward, as I pushed her in the plastic bassinet down the hall.

April 13

We called her Anna because we liked that name, the sound of it, and because Beth's sister's name is Ann. We gave her my own last name, a somewhat twisted version of the French "l'oiseau," meaning "the bird." It might have been a hard last name for Anna to live with. I can't prove this, of course, but it must be among the most misspelled and mispronounced names in America. Still, "It has character," my parents always said. "It says where you come from."

My paternal forebears were farmers in northern France, some of whom ended up in Iowa, farming again, and spreading the gospel, Baptist-style. With the dust bowl, my great-grandparents came east, still with the gospel and the work ethic, but without the farm. They started small businesses that prospered and grew, and now are by-and-large defunct. There was a linen importing company that my father inherited and has recently closed up. And there were hardware stores, lumber yards, and building operations.

It is pure egoism, but I am very proud that Anna shared my last name. It speaks of a mixed heritage of suffering and failure and hard-earned success. All those farmers and merchants and peddlers of Christian theology. Proud and intolerant, suspicious of pleasure, steel-willed and nostalgic. In my family there is deep resentment and deepest love. In part, it is where Anna came from, and where I come from. And where *all this* is probably founded.

April 14

For the record — and with a little embarrassment — I should list Anna's other names, the nicknames we called her. Beth's favorites were: Pumpkin, Pumpkin-dunkin, Pumpkin-pie. Mine were: Snuggins, Snuggo, Snuggarroo, Snuggins-buggins; and we both called her Anna-banana.

We still call her these names, and I hope we never forget them, for in my own mind at least, they refer mostly to that playful and mischievous part of her personality. In the months before she died, Anna must have known her various names, or recognized the tones in which we said them. I would come into the family room and she would be rocking in her swing. I would say in my own silly, mischievous tone, "Anna? Anna-banana?" And she would turn and give me that smile, and kick her legs and clutch her hands beneath her chin.

When Anna died, we were left with her toys, clothes, the medical bills, the box of ashes, and all of our memories. Yet perhaps most powerfully, we were left with her name: an arrangement of letters, a word, a sound on our lips that is everything.

We called her Anna. We said that word when she was born. And I remember in those hours when she was dying, and when that strange animal sound came unwilled from the deepest part of me. What the sound said was my daughter's name. I was calling her name, over and over. And in the days after her death, we lay on our bed and called and called her name. We still call her name. It is all we can do. It is all that we have to throw at the sky.

April 15

Easter. And this morning I read in Matthew, Mark, Luke, and John, the stories of the crucifixion, the empty tomb, and Jesus' appearances, after his death, before the disciples. I don't believe all this, as believers must believe it. I have no way of knowing that a God exists, or that a Son of God existed, or that such a being could rise from the dead. Still, I am moved by the story, by the barbarity of crucifixion, and what must have been his suffering.

I find myself responding much more to the man part of Jesus than to the god part of him. When (in Matthew and Mark) he cries as he is dying, "My God, why hast thou forsaken me?" — that is a man speaking. A question, a fear, a profound doubt is his final word.

As for his resurrection, I am all agog. It is wonderful, but I am more doubting than Thomas. What does it mean to rise from the dead? How does it happen? So far as I can tell, the dead can only arise in the minds of the living, in an act of imagination. And that is good for the living. Just as it is good for me that I can imagine Anna, or remember her so intensely as to feel her in my arms.

But again, what does that do for her? Where does that leave her?

We are told that Christ's death was good for humankind, but I keep wondering what it was for him, as a man; or what it was for his mother, who is but briefly mentioned in the gospels. Why is so little said of his pain? Why don't we even see her tears?

I think we are tricking ourselves with all this talk about resurrection. It makes it easier to forget that a person has actually died, and that people do die — painfully, randomly, and for no reason at all. If there is meaning in any of this — and I think there must be — it is in the living and the dying, and not in some supposed life after the dying.

That is why *this* is all so important. Though I wish I could believe otherwise, Anna lived and then she died. She is in no other *place*. She is gone absolutely, and that is all there is — except for these things we can hold in our minds.

April 17

Last year, on April 11, we brought Anna into the Pediatric Clinic at Georgetown Hospital for her weekly EKG, oxygen saturation test, antibiotic injection, and catheterized urine analysis. On the following morning, she was admitted to the hospital for a cardiac catheterization, scheduled for noon. The procedure, though usually performed on adults and not without danger, is common in most major hospitals. Under general anesthesia, a tube, or catheter, is fed into the femoral vein in the thigh, and, with doctors watching with ultrasound, the tube is snaked all the way up to and into the heart. There a dye is released and a clear image of the heart in action (much clearer than an echocardiogram) can be recorded on X-ray film.

By 11:00 A.M. everything was ready to go. Anna was on a prophylactic IV antibiotic: the familiar click of the IVAC pump, the bag on the pole, the dangling tubing, and the needle in the top of her hand. We were in a room in the Pediatric Step-Down Unit. It must have been on the east side of the building, for the clear spring sun came through the window, and I remember squinting in the way that I do when it is bright, when my contacts are dry, and I haven't had enough sleep.

Incredibly, and sadly, I can't remember in any great detail what Anna looked like that day. I know she was beginning to look more pale, a bluish tinge around her mouth and nose when she was upset. And I also recall her seeming a little more lethargic about that time. Yet I'm afraid that what I see now is only a generalized image of her on that morning. I can't swear by it, but her eyes must have had that uncertain look that came when she was scared or in a strange place. It was probably the same look that was in our own eyes.

For what I *do* remember is the taste of stale coffee in a styrofoam cup, and that strange unquenchable thirst that I often have when I am afraid. I don't care how many times you have seen a child through surgery or how routine the procedure, it is always a fearful moment when the nurses come to take your child away, and it is always a fearful wait until you see your child smiling again.

In a way, some part of me is still waiting for that smile, still pacing the blue-carpeted halls on C6-2, Cardiac Intensive Care; still sitting for a moment and trying to read Chekhov's "A Dreary Story," then getting up and going to the water fountain, pacing once more, and listening for the phone to ring — all this while Anna was six

floors down, her body chilled, her heart laid open in a blaze of light. I
am still waiting to see her smile again.

April 18

But on that morning last April there would be no waiting like
that. Shortly before the cardiac catheterization was to begin, Dr.
Shapiro, who was to perform the operation, came into our room and I
recall him saying, "Well, not today." The lab results from Anna's
urinalysis, despite her daily oral antibiotics, showed another large
urinary tract infection. At this time, the cardiac cath would be much
too risky. Instead, Anna was to begin another course of IV antibiotics
for at least a week, or until the infection was under control. Then Dr.
Shapiro would try again.

At first I was relieved that the procedure was not to be immediately performed, and then there was the prospect of Anna and Beth
spending another week or more in the hospital. With the nurses, we
wheeled Anna down to the pediatric wing, where she was set up with
her IV in a room with another sick infant girl and her mother. I
remember a lot of paperwork that had to be signed; and later that
afternoon, after Anna's IV had stopped working, there was a terrible
hour in a small examining room, where a doctor and two nurses had
trouble getting another needle into a vein in Anna's foot. She
screamed and screamed; I held the oxygen tube to her nose. The veins
stood out on her forehead, and I had never seen her face turn so blue.
Beth had to leave for a while, and then it got to the point where I
couldn't stand it, and I remember asking the doctor to stop, to leave us
alone. It just all seemed too much.

Without getting the needle in, they all left, Beth returned, and
with the door shut we were in there, just the three of us — I think all
of us in tears.

April 19

It is like an animal feeling — when all you want is to be alone as
a family, to burrow into a small place, when even the hospital seems

like a greater threat than any disease or disability. We must have kept the door shut for a half hour in that examining room. Nobody bothered us. No one even knocked. I remember Beth was finally able to nurse Anna, and that seemed to calm us all. Eventually I went out and told the doctor that we were ready. Again I would hold Anna while he got the needle in, assembled the heparin lock, and wrapped her foot with tape and gauze. Then we got her settled in her room.

From our pediatrician, we learned of a company that provides all the equipment for at-home IV antibiotic care; and for the rest of that afternoon one of us was on the phone, making arrangements and making sure that our insurance company would foot the bill. That night Beth stayed at the hospital with Anna, and on the next morning, I was here to receive all the IV equipment in addition to an "oxygen concentrator" and a portable oxygen tank, which our doctors recommended that we have on hand. About midmorning I returned to the hospital to bring Beth and Anna home.

April 20

When I think of that period (April 13-24) when Anna was at home on IV antibiotics, my mind goes up our stairs and settles in her small room, on the poster bed, where I would be sitting and watching the clear antibiotic dripping from the hanging bag. Beth would be in the corner chair, and having nursed Anna, would be rocking her now in her arms, the pole beside them, the tube snaking down and the needle disappearing into the catheter in Anna's foot. Now and then I would get up and adjust the roller clamp or change the position of Anna's leg to make the drip go faster or slower. I'd check the needle in the heprin lock. Then I'd sit again on the bed.

Three times a day we did this, about forty-five minutes each time, as the medicine dripped into Anna's veins. I can't say that I particularly enjoyed it. I'm not exactly a patient person, and as Beth says, I have a "hard time relaxing," or doing what is apparently nothing. But what I think I am learning is that there are times of quiet vigilance, of caring, or watching, or simply being, that drop by drop amount to more than I could have ever imagined.

So much of my life I have spent in trying to be productive: in school, teaching, or even on these last two afternoons, as I have been madly sledge-hammering a concrete stairway off our back porch in order to build a new, more pleasing, wooden one. I don't begrudge these activities. I will always do them, and to some extent, I have to do them. Yet I am surprised by how little of this actually remains when your life at some point makes you weigh up its worth.

What I remember, and what moves me, about our time with Anna was not what we might have produced, but simply the way that we were, the three of us — or that we were at all. That is what takes my breath away. Those times of sitting on the bed, or beside the isolette, the times of just being there, like keeping watch, when nothing was dramatically done or achieved, when all we were doing, unbeknownst to us then, was making these memories that can now help us live.

April 22

10:00 P.M.: This is one of those evenings that marks the change of season. Thus far, it has been a cool and wet April, though tonight, with my window open for the first time this year and the sound of neighbors' voices on front porches, you have the sense that something has turned, that things will never be exactly the same. Outside the temperature is in the low sixties. Cars go by, and I can hear their radios. Through the screen, the air is still and sweet with the scent of grass that I have just mown this evening. It reminds me of my childhood, that smell. And so do these stains that make the soles of my sneakers green.

Late this afternoon, we returned from a two-day trip to my parents' home, where, as a kid, it was my job to cut the grass. Now, because my father is no longer well enough to sit on his riding mower, they have somebody else do it, a professional outfit that also fertilizes and sweeps the leaves in the fall. At any rate, as soon as we got back here, I revved up the mower and pushed it back and forth on the lawn. It is a bourgeois pleasure that I freely admit to: the look and smell of smooth-cut grass. For four summers while I was in college I worked on a golf course, pushing a greens mower or driving a tractor with a gang of mowers behind me. To see a winding, freshly cut fairway, or even our tiny backyard, where I have edged the flower beds and my new-sown grass is growing in the bare spots: it speaks to me of a small and fragile order. Illusory perhaps. But it feels good to see some things in their places, some things that are green and alive.

April 23

While Anna was on at-home IV antibiotics, there was one disturbing night when the IV didn't flow correctly, and we had to take her into the Emergency Room so a doctor could put another catheter into a larger vein in her foot. Again it was excruciating for Anna, but when the pain was over and she was home, it was almost as if nothing had happened. She was cheerful. To keep her foot warm, we stretched a sock over all the gauze, the catheter and heparin lock. I can see her now, smiling and kicking in her swing, with what seemed like a big white boot on her slender leg.

Around her IV infusions, we were able to live our normal lives, or pretty much the lives we had envisioned for ourselves as parents. If anything, Anna might have been easier than most infants. She never had colic. She went to bed at exactly 8:00 P.M. almost every night, and seldom did she cry for extended periods of time. As for us, I wrote or prepared my class in the mornings, often with Anna rocking in the swing. On some afternoons, between nursings, Beth went to meetings at school, and on weekends we'd take Anna with us to visit friends, or go to the restaurant at the end of our street. Then, by this date last year, another urinalysis showed that Anna's infection had cleared up, and her cardiac catheterization was rescheduled for April 25.

April 25

On the morning of Anna's cardiac catheterization, she weighed 3.8 kilograms, or 8.36 pounds, and measured 21 inches long. I know this because a year ago Beth wrote it on our baby calendar, which I have on my desk. Every Tuesday Anna was weighed and measured at the beginning of her appointments with the cardiologists, and how I remember laying her, pink and naked, on that scale, and then laying her in the wooden box where the nurse would stretch her out, all reedlike, narrow-hipped, and read the number, head to heel.

What a thing it is to see your child laid out naked on a hard surface. It is almost unspeakable, such vulnerability and openness. And just as unspeakable: that feeling of scooping her up again, holding all of that nakedness again in your arms, even if she was urinating, warm and wet, all over your shirt.

The cardiac catheterization was successfully performed, even though, before she was anesthetized on the operating table, Anna had one of her big blue spells that delayed the procedure for a while. Again, my memory is fuzzy, though I do recall that moment when they brought her back to her room. Once more she was lying behind the glass of a wheeled isolette, with the monitors going and the sound of her heart beating. The nurses lifted her onto the crib, keeping the wires and tubes untangled. We could touch her and hold her hand, and that was good — though still there was such a terrific distance when she was under the anesthetic. It might have looked about the same, but this sort of unconsciousness felt so much deeper and more inaccessible than sleep. I couldn't have known it then, but when I remember it now, it feels more like death than it feels like sleep: when your hand cannot bring a child awake.

April 26

But Anna would awaken that evening, groggy, still on morphine, but recovering well enough. Then on the next morning when I came into the hospital, I remember walking down the hall and stopping in my tracks before I even got to Anna's door. What stopped me was a familiar though wholly unexpected sound: her loud cooing that we would hear at home, so suddenly exotic in a place like this. When I went in she was on her back in the crib, kicking her legs, and Beth, who had stayed with her that night, was bent over her, engaged in "conversation." I don't think I had ever heard Anna so loud and happy, and this less than a day after she had lain there so anesthetized and distant.

It makes me smile to remember this, and this should be one of those memories that I really hold on to. From the doorway I could see them both outlined against the open venetian blinds. Slender Beth was busty with nursing. She was laughing and shaking her head at Anna and making her mouth and eyes go big. Anna was simply beside herself with delight, still on the IV, but kicking like crazy, the plastic IV tube swinging this way and that. I remember that nurses came in to see what all the laughter was about. And I can still see those bars of sunlight on the linoleum floor, and Beth operating a "Busy Box" for Anna to see, a toy with movable gadgets and all sorts of dinging and ratcheting noises.

But mostly I remember that birdlike sound of Anna's giggling and the way it wove with Beth's deeper laughter, and the way that all of that made me feel.

There were these moments of euphoria during Anna's life, often on the heels of our deepest concerns. There was almost a rhythm to it, her way of coming through danger and then finding her greatest joy in the most unlikely of circumstances. When I think of her life, I must remember this too: that with tubes in her veins, her eyes could still be delighted. She could kick her legs. She could cry with pleasure, filling the halls, even in the place where she would die.

April 30

The pregnancy test that Beth had today was negative, so again we're disappointed, though not despairing. We begin another round of Perganol injections, ultrasounds, and blood tests this week.

May 1

There is a sadness each time that another month begins and I turn another page of the calendar. More and more there is that sense of Anna sliding away. And more and more there is this: the feeling that some months from now, like her life itself, all of this writing must come to an end. Not a conclusion, but an end: some place where the writing stops, where I turn a page and Anna has died, even in the retelling — and there is no more story to give.

I don't know exactly when this time will come, though I sense its lumbering approach. And I fear it, too, for it must mark some point of letting go, of loosening my grip, acknowledging it, and feeling her floating even farther away.

It occurs to me now that this could be more difficult than I might have foreseen. Because when an only child dies, you are terribly lost — except for the circle of your spouse's arms, and perhaps, if you are lucky, some strange mooring such as *this*.

It has become a ritual to me now, this sitting here and remembering Anna. There is pain, but there is also the slow pleasure of getting it down, the accumulation of pages, however flawed and incomplete, day after day, morning after morning, as if there is something in this world that is almost predictable.

I wish this wasn't my story to tell. I wish there were no story at all. I would give anything to erase these pages and have Anna — she'd be walking by now! — toddling around this room. But I have no alternative. This is the situation. I can write of nothing more knowledgeably than the life I have lived. Right now I can hardly imagine writing anything else, or what I will do when this comes to an end.

Before we brought Anna home after the cardiac catheterization, Dr. Shapiro took us down to a small darkened room in the cath lab where we saw the new film of Anna's heart. He ran it at varying speeds, backward and forward. It was in black and white, just a minute or two long, and yet I can remember it almost exactly. The first thing we saw was the catheter itself, a thin white line, like a needle and thread, working its way through the inferior vena cava.

When it entered the right atrium, it released some dye, and suddenly the whole right side of Anna's heart (to the left as we looked at it) was as clear as those cross-sectional diagrams that you've seen in anatomy textbooks. Only this heart was bigger; and moving, really moving, clenching and releasing, the dye flooding through the flapping valve and swirling wildly before most of it shot through the pulmonary artery.

For a moment I had the impression that I was looking straight up at the sky, as when the clouds are fast and whirling and for a moment you lose your balance. This was *inside* my daughter's heart. It seemed preposterous, or fictional, as in Asimov's *Fantastic Voyage*, which I read as a kid. Yet there it all was, terribly vivid: the hole between her ventricles and the hourglass narrowing of her pulmonary artery. We watched as the catheter threaded *through* the hole between her atria and released more dye on the left side. It seemed so clear and un-impeachable, all of these defects, all of this trouble — and still her heart beat so wildly.

Like a needle and thread.

By the time the catheter had finished its meanderings and the film paused, Anna's heart seemed like some of my mother's sewing, a bit of folded cloth, something half mended and left on a chair where she had hastily gotten up.

In the end, Anna's heart *would* be mended in much the same way: the holes patched and stitched closed, a thin thread drawn through a muscle. So too had her throat been mended, and the incisions sewn up along the sides of her chest, and then the one down the center of her breastbone, and inside of that the incision that had opened her heart itself.

All these layers of mending, stitch after stitch, scar over scar; and every thread held; no muscle tore.

By these finest filaments are we held together. Rent tissue is sewn and heals; scars cover the wounds.

And yet this is what is so hard to swallow; this is what really gets me: Anna died while she was healing. The threads held, but something gave. A heart can stop when it is strongest.

May 3

4:30 A.M.: It has been some months since I have been wide awake at this time of the night — or morning, really. It is pitch dark outside. Jessie sleeps on the rug. There are no cars on the road, but already a bird is trilling wildly outside my window, as if it knows something the rest of us don't. About five minutes ago, while I was making coffee, I heard a train rumbling in the distance, the familiar moo of its whistle, like the call of an old friend.

When I got out of bed, Beth asked from her sleep, "What's going on?"

I said, "I can't sleep. I'm going downstairs."

"Are you thinking about her?"

I said yes. Though the truth of it is that I was thinking more about myself than Anna, more about how her life and death have affected me — or rather, how I have responded.

I am aware that my response is not altogether flattering to me. I have turned more deeply inward. And I know that some of my friends — particularly my longtime friends, most of whom never met Anna — must find this awkward and troublesome. There are letters that I have not answered and letters that I have not even opened. For six months, a stack of manuscripts has lain untouched beside my radiator — friends' manuscripts that I said I would read, that I *meant* to read and have had time to read, though I suspect I will send them back unread, with a note that says, "I am sorry."

Somehow I haven't had it in me to do such things. I haven't the energy. Or perhaps I am beyond the point of caring. I can't imagine responding to these letters. How do I begin to say how we "are doing"? How do I respond to these photos of their pink-cheeked children?

Yes, I am selfish. And I envy my friends' parenthood. I quake at the scrawled and awkward ABCDEFG on the back of a photo, and the ragged outline of a heart, a valentine, drawn in a child's hand, a daughter's hand: a heart made with a hand.

It is all so well-intended, so innocent, and still it tears me apart. I feel the child's effort and concentration to hold the hand steady, to draw a straight line, to make some shape that makes some sense.

When I have some spare time, I don't write letters or read these manuscripts. Instead, I miter and nail new moldings in our living room and dining room, and more recently I have built a staircase and railing that leads off our back porch to the yard. The old one was concrete and dangerously precipitous — several times Beth nearly tripped carrying Anna down there. But this new one I've built is solid. All pressure treated two-by stock; 16d galvanized flooring nails. And the rise is gradual (seven inches per eleven-inch treads), easy to climb and descend.

It takes me a while, for I am not a carpenter, but it feels good to build a simple thing, and then to actually stand on it and feel its substance beneath my feet. Right now I can't stand on those letters that I should have written, or my obligations to those from whom I feel suddenly distant.

I can only stand on these things I can make, even though I know there is some madness in all of this building, as though I can nail together, board by board, some thing that can replace what is lost.

There is gray light in my window now. It's a cool cloudy morning, and soon we are to go to the hospital for Beth's blood test, that will tell us how she's responding this month to her Pergonal treatments. I can hear her upstairs, running water in the sink. Beside me, Jessie is stirring and stretching, and I am about to let her out the back door, where she'll trot down my new stairs to relieve herself in the grass. Perhaps some day we'll carry another child up and down those stairs, and perhaps later we'll hear that child's own light step and a hand sliding on the railing. There will be pleasure in that. And a deep pang of remembering. I hope that's the way it will be.

May 7

Over last weekend, we returned to the nursery where many months ago we bought Anna's tree. This time we bought some flower seedlings for the small garden in our front yard and for the window boxes, three of which hang outside Anna's room. About a year and a half ago, I built those flower boxes and gave them to Beth for Christmas. She was eight months pregnant with Anna at the time, and I was somehow enraptured by the vision of flower boxes outside a child's dormer windows, as if I could make some English country house of this squat bungalow in Hyattsville.

About a month after that Christmas, Anna was born, and during the following April, a little more than a year ago, I painted the boxes white. Next I drilled and screwed in the metal supporting brackets beneath Anna's windows. Then at the very end of April we filled each box with potting soil and planted impatiens. All through last May, the impatiens grew, and standing about eight inches high, each a small hill of blossoms, they almost filled the bottom half of Anna's windows. Toward the middle of June, though, when the weather turned hot and muggy, they began to grow leggy and some of the leaves turned yellow. Still they blossomed, and they were blossoming when, at the end of June, we took Anna to Georgetown for her heart surgery.

During that week, we stayed at the hospital while one of our parents ferried provisions from home. All of our energy and attention were focused on Anna, who lay transformed beneath the orange heat lamps, with all the machines going. And yet even then, as Anna lay dying, I remember asking my mother to make sure, when she returned to our house, that she watered the flowers in the window boxes.

Then on the Fourth of July, after we had held Anna for the last time and laid her back on those crisp white sheets, I remember driving up to our house in a drizzling rain, and looking up above our front porch, and seeing all the blossoms, those soft mounds of color, in the white boxes beneath her windows.

May 8

Yesterday at the hospital, we saw on ultrasound eight eggs forming in Beth's ovaries, four on each side, a few of them almost mature. In the swirling haze of her abdomen, they were clear and round, their sides slightly wobbling, like glass molten on the blower's pipe.

So much wonder, it seems, is lost or unborn. So much is so hard to breathe a life into. What there is is the trying, and the living of the trying. The rest is out of our hands.

May 10

My sister Meg, her husband, and their two sons have recently arrived in Washington for a week-long business/vacation stay. Last evening they all came over here, and then we went into town for dinner. Paul, their older son, an eight-year-old, has recently gotten a new camera (a present, as it turns out, from my mother), which he wears like a talisman around his neck. As we sat down to dinner, he made us all smile and say cheese as the flash went off. Then he and I exchanged places, and I took the camera, so that he could be included, front and center, in the next photo.

As I squatted down and framed the faces in the small glass rectangle, I felt vaguely awkward, as though I didn't altogether know what I was doing, or I couldn't find the right button to push. Now this morning as I think about it, I realize that neither Beth nor I have taken a picture since Anna was alive — not since I shot that photo of Anna in Beth's arms, as she looked straight at the camera, her eyes so wide and surprised, on that morning in our kitchen before we took her in for her heart surgery.

Historically, we have not been big picture-takers. Some parts of our lives are chronicled in albums that now stand on my bookshelves: our trips to the Adirondacks, various family get-togethers, our wedding eight years ago on Piseco Lake, our travels in England, and moving into our new (that is, old) house. It is a spotty record at best. Yet when Anna arrived — as this stack of photos here will attest — the camera was often clicking.

While Anna was alive, Beth put the earliest photos (of Anna's first month) in two small albums. Since her death, though, we have been unable to arrange the rest of the photos, about a hundred of them, in the album we had bought some months ago for that purpose. It has to do, I think, with having to put them in some particular order, between two covers, with a beginning and an end. That just

163

seems so hard right now. As if we'd be making some book we could close and put away on the shelf.

I don't know when, if ever, we can arrange this album. I don't know when, if ever, we can say something ends. In the meantime, I doubt that we will take many photos. What would we take them *of*? There is Beth. There are family and friends. Yet so much now seems so invisible; so much that matters seems so invisible.

May 11

On May 9, 10, and 11 last year, we took Anna into the hospital for three separate doctor's appointments. The first was her weekly exam with one of her cardiologists, and the third, which I will get to shortly, was our initial meeting with Dr. Hopkins to discuss Anna's forthcoming heart surgery. The second was a final visit to Dr. Hoy, who looked at the scars on the sides of Anna's chest, and then at her throat. It seemed that her throat had completely mended, his job was done, and this child who was born unable to eat would someday soon swallow solid food.

That was the last time we would see Dr. Hoy, until he came up to Cardiac Intensive Care during one of Anna's last days. He had no official reason to go up there. Anna was no longer under his charge. He had just come to look in on a patient whom months before he had helped to live.

On that day I remember seeing him talking earnestly with a group of Anna's doctors outside her door. He is a straightforward, all-business doctor with his square glasses and square jaw. He was studying a lab report in his brown sport jacket, the front unbuttoned, when I went out and said hello. As always, there was little to say, and that we said awkwardly. Finally he said, "Good luck," with neither optimism nor pessimism, but with that strange, slightly squinting look that meant he was holding back whatever he felt.

Six months later, in December, we would run into him again on that day we returned to the hospital to talk to Drs. Hopkins, Beder, and Gibbons about the autopsy report. We were walking down a hall

164

when Dr. Hoy came out of a doorway, walking fast, heading some-where, with something on his mind. For an instant he didn't recog-nize us, and then he did. He stopped and shook hands. I recall thanking him again for all he had done for Anna, and over his face came that same awkward squinting look, so strange in a big blocky man. After a moment he said, "I'm sorry she died." And after another moment, "I have to go."

The last I remember of this man who opened Anna's stomach on the day she was born, who sewed up her throat and esophagus ten days later, who held her heart in the palm of his hand, who mended her so that she could live — the last we saw of him was the back of his jacket as he strode like a commuter down that hall. He must have been going to the Intermediate Nursery or the ICN. Or down to surgery, where another child would be splayed in the light, and he would wash his thick hands.

May 12

Hands. How often I seem to see them. Anna's long, tapered fingers and thumbs; the way they would close and unfold, reach and grasp, clumsy claws, two thumbs in the mouth; fingers entwined when she was happy; or slack in sleep, or clenched in pain, holding.

It is Dr. Hopkins's hands, too, that I most remember on that next morning, May 11, a year ago. It was our first appointment with him, and we would ask questions, and he would describe to us, step by step, the delicate surgery for mending Anna's heart. He is a bearish man with sloped shoulders and a soft voice. He has bushy eyebrows, hair in his ears, and his hands are large, his fingers as thick as Dr. Hoy's, though not so blunt at the ends. His nails are wide and trimmed, and I remember the thick strands of gray hair just above his knuckles where he wore his wedding ring.

I remember all this because in the next two months we would often see his hands as they helped explain a procedure, as they drew a picture, or as one of them stroked Anna's hair, or adjusted a dial, or pointed to the monitors, or helped him think while supporting his chin, or made a fist, or finally as he held them out, side by side, his palms upturned — those wide hands so empty.

But on that day in his office, it was the ribbed top of his right hand that I would see, as he felt the bones of Anna's chest — ribs and sternum, the narrow place where his hand would enter. Anna was in Beth's arms at the time, and we had unbuttoned the front of her shirt. His hand, extended, was wider than all of her chest. It was thick and veined, yet it moved with delicacy, softly searching as over braille.

We had done our research regarding Dr. Hopkins, and we had found, through an uncle of mine who works at New York Hospital, that he was one of the best heart surgeons around. That was reassuring. And yet it was his hands, in the end, that most comforted me: a father's hands, all grained and gnarled. And the way they moved on my daughter's skin, gently and without fear.

May 13

Mother's Day. And difficult, especially for Beth.

My two nephews have been staying here for the past two days, their sleeping bags strewn on my study floor, their children's sounds filling our house. This morning, when I returned with the boys from the park, I went upstairs and found Beth crying in Anna's room. She was sitting in the rocker, and — this, after what I have recently been thinking — she was putting the first photos of Anna in the new album. She was only able to put in a few, and I didn't have it in me to put in any more. We looked at the photos of Anna in her isolette, and the ones where we held her in our arms.

How many times have I looked at those photos with all of my being still reaching in through the plastic portals? I trace an eyebrow, an ear, smooth back the furry hair.

"I can practically touch her," Beth said, over and over. "I can practically touch her."

Tonight, after the boys have gone and our house is quiet, I take the small brass candlestick from the mantelpiece, set it on the dining room table, and we eat our dinner in the wavering glow. We say there was much light in Anna's life: the shimmering trees, the chandelier, the candles. And we say there was also much pain. We think that the light outshone the pain; and we think that such life, however short, is good.

But the death of that life is intolerably bad, as bad as the life is good. For the death of a child is the death of potential, the death of a whole life unlived, the death of light itself.

Now I write these words in the glow of that candle, and I know that the glow is a kind of consumption, that the flame stands on the ashy wick. I know that something must die for something else to burn with life. That is "Nature," I am told, or a turn of the "Wheel of Life." Life follows death, which follows life, which follows death. . . .

But something is wrong here. This is the death of a child. What possible good can outweigh what is lost? What flame outglow a full life lived?

What is best burned is a life full-spent, the dried husk, and not the shooting seed. You cannot make order of a child's death. These splintered bones can spoke no wheel. This feather of light is not the sun.

May 16

I have found, in the jumbled pile of papers and receipts beneath our kitchen telephone, the business card of Dr. Hopkins. On the front it is just what you'd expect: an embossed university emblem in the upper left-hand corner, and in the middle his name and degree. Below that it reads, "Pediatric and Adult Cardiothoracic Surgery"; then there is an address and phone number. On the back, though, are some hastily scrawled notes, most in my own handwriting, that go every which way. They seem to be in no particular order, though I have ordered them here:

A neg 15 donors
one important — close if pos.

cross-matched
use on day

June 8-18 (out of town) [This in Dr. Hopkins's writing]

July 26th

When I look at these notes and think about them, I am almost transported back to that small office, with the reassurance of Dr. Hopkins's hands and Anna in our arms; and yet the apprehension that something was really happening here, whatever was coming was under way — something necessary and unavoidable, and dangerous.

Anna's chest, he said, would be opened with a vertical incision though her breastbone, and her ribs would be pushed apart. Her body temperature would be lowered, and she would be put on a heart-lung machine that would pump blood through her system while her own heart was stilled. Then her heart itself would be opened. I don't remember in what order it was to happen, but a single stitch would close the hole between her atria; a patch would be sewn over the hole between her ventricles; the pulmonary valve would be slit so that it opened wider; and the hard muscle that constricted her pulmonary artery would be cut away. Next, her heart would be sewn up, and the leads to an emergency pacemaker implanted. She would be taken off the heart-lung machine and her heart restarted. Then her chest would be sewn back together, and she would be brought back up to Cardiac Intensive Care.

In all, the operation would be about six or seven hours, and we should be warned that when we would see her afterward, she would be unconscious, swollen, and her skin would be pale and cold. She would be on a respirator. There would be monitors. There could be five or more IV lines into her arms.

If all went well, she would be in Intensive Care for about a week, and then another week in the Pediatric Step-Down Unit. Dr. Hopkins had performed this procedure on children from one day old to two or three years. For a six-month-old, the chance for success was 95 percent. Barring any unusual circumstances, her heart would never have to be fixed again. She would grow, and she would live, like any other child.

I realize as I write this that I have been trying to be as cool and clinical as I was trying to be as we sat in the office and Dr. Hopkins told us all this, even showed us a valve from a human heart, and how he would cut it — a whitish butterfly thing in a clear bag of formaldehyde. I wanted to see and know all of this. I wanted to hold in my mind the entire procedure, follow its logic, step by step, and see it through to its probable end.

Somehow I still feel this way, as if there is something else I must try to understand, something I've missed or overseen — even though I know that in the end it all flies apart, the monitors go crazy, and there is nothing in the world that I can do about it.

May 17

Concerning those notes on the back of the business card: Anna's blood type was A negative, and the compatible blood of approximately fifteen donors would be used during the surgery. If we had any family or friends with such blood, it could be donated directly for Anna's use. Furthermore, a unit of fresh whole blood, given within forty-eight hours before the surgery, would be necessary for clotting purposes at the end of the operation. Because the matching here was especially critical, this fresh blood, if possible, should come from either parent or the closest family member.

As it turned out, neither Beth nor I have Anna's blood type. Nor do any of our friends or family, except my mother, who had her blood tested in New Jersey, and later cross-matched with Anna's blood down here at Georgetown last June 22. It was a good match, the lab reported, and I remember a kind of exhilaration in knowing that my mother, who had seen me through many operations as a child, would be contributing directly to Anna's well-being.

169

So on the afternoon of June 26, the day before we took Anna into the hospital for her surgery, my mother, who wouldn't tell the nurse her age, would lie on a bed in the blood lab, in her crisp white blouse with a silver pin, and her navy blue pleated skirt pulled tight to her legs. She had her red pumps, the color of her lipstick, side by side on the floor. She clutched her purse in her left arm, and in her right was the needle and the tube where her dark blood flowed into the bag with Anna's name typed on the label.

I don't think I'm straying far from the facts when I say that my mother, who isn't usually crazy about infants, took a special interest in Anna — perhaps because of Anna's medical problems and the way she responded, and perhaps, too, because of a certain thin-boned fragility that is evident in the childhood pictures of my mother as well. In any event, it has often come back to me, and with something like awe, that my daughter died with some part of my mother's blood in her veins and heart.

The dates on the back of the business card are pretty straightforward. Dr. Hopkins would be out of town, on vacation, from June 8 through the 18th, though in case of an emergency (a severe cyanotic spell), he would return to perform the surgery. If, on the other hand, there were no surprises, the operation would go ahead as scheduled for Wednesday, July 26, just a few days after Anna would be six months old.

May 18

Today I read in the paper that after a week-long search, the wreck of a small plane and the bodies of six men were found in a remote hardwood forest in Spotsylvania County, Virginia, about ten miles south of Lake Anna, a place I noted some months ago in these pages. In the early morning of May 10, the men were returning to the Washington area from a fishing expedition in North Carolina. They left Manteo, North Carolina about 1:30 A.M., and the pilot made his last radio contact near Richmond. At 2:50 A.M. the last radar blip was recorded, showing the plane at eight-hundred feet. Then it disappeared from the screens.

There were no storms in the immediate area, no lightning, and there was no evidence of fire. The pilot was experienced; the plane's maintenance record was up-to-date. The wreckage, spread over a five-hundred-square-yard area and some of it dangling from trees, appeared to have fallen almost straight down from the sky. The fuselage struck the ground at a sixty-degree angle, "causing serious damage to only one large tree, which was uprooted and dragged 50 feet."

An "inflight breakup" is what they are calling it. The cause unknown. Six men are flying along, something breaks for no apparent reason, and they are spiraling down, hitting the earth, a single tree felled by their lives.

It is so ridiculous and undignified, this death we are coming to — our limp bodies thrown from the wreckage. We held Anna like this, and now I think I know: it is not the world's order that makes us love; nor is it some beneficent God. Rather, it is his absence, the chaos, the sense that at any moment we can fall from the sky. That is what makes us hold all the harder.

May 23
PISECO, NEW YORK. MIDAFTERNOON

I am writing this about fifty feet from the edge of Piseco Lake, in Beth's parents' tent-trailer where Beth and I have found some refuge from all the relatives and the blackflies. She is napping in the cot behind me, and through the screen beside her, I can see the pale blue of the lake and the gentle rise of the mountain, shaped like an owl's head. The leaves up here are just beginning to come out, and so the deciduous trees have that frail and diaphanous look. Except for the pines, the mountain is a soft yellow-green.

We are here for a four-day vacation. And perhaps like the trumpeter swans, we have come north once more to a place of beginnings, beside this lake, and in the shade of this mountain where we were married, and where two years ago Anna was conceived. Now we wait again for a sign. Beth's period is late. So we watch the clouds and the squalling waves. There are deer tracks in the sand and tiny bluets in the fields. The water, we all say, is higher than ever; just look at the waves lapping over the docks. Is it some kind of abundance? Or an unwanted excess — these streams so swollen with rain?

May 24
DUSK

There is something in the way that a large lake holds light. When it is dark on the land and dark in the sky, there is still some light in the lake. Tonight was a beautiful sunset, the ribbed undersides of the clouds all orange and violet, the water sleeked, as though oiled and iridescent. For so long the lake held that color against the blackness of the shore and the dimming sky. It held it in all of its width and depth, and holds it even now as the electric lights on the opposite shore shine their little swaths across the surface.

We have just come in from a short canoe trip around the island, a sad trip, I'm afraid, for in the bathroom before dinner we knew what we suspected: another month has gone by, another birth date missed, another sign of nothing to come.

Last year at this time, we'd be putting Anna to bed. And last year at this time, we'd be patting her back until her body relaxed, and then her breathing eased, and then we'd quietly go out her door.

Now as I look out on this lake beneath the starless sky, I wonder if we can hold what light there is in us. I see the big rounded mountain and the dark shoreline, and I hear the peepers, like mad bells along the cold-rushing stream. When we were out on the lake, we could hear almost anything: that way sound carries on the wide water. It was utterly still. We were in the middle of the lake, in all that vastness, and for a time we didn't even move our paddles.

You would have thought that then, if ever, we might have heard Anna's breath, or the breath of a life unknown — if it was out there, anywhere, on some other shore. What we heard instead were the

172

sounds of people in their cottages, and the campers far away on the beach, their guitars and low voices around a fire.

Tonight will be chilly again: four quilts, socks, and my flannel shirt. On the crate beside our sleeping bags, Beth has set the picture of Anna that she usually has on her bedside table at home. It is the one in the frame that I gave her for Christmas, the one with Anna holding a toy frog and wearing those sea-green booties, tied with ribbons, that Beth had knitted her last spring.

When we get under these quilts tonight, we'll look at that picture, and there will be nothing new we can say. We remember her hair, her eyes, the smoothness of her skin. We remember the feel of picking her up, the smell of her neck, and the warm weight of her over our shoulders.

May 28
MEMORIAL DAY
DAWN

It is 6:00 A.M., or shortly thereafter. I have gotten up early, and I am sitting out here on the beach with the heaps of mundungus, the leaves of last summer, washed up on the edge of the glassy water. The sky is clear. The sun is on the horizon and shining full-force against this side of the mountain. In the days we have been here, the leaves have emerged, and the mountain has lost that fragile look. Out by the island, a band of mist is rising, and near the west shore, Beth's father's boat, a Boston Whaler, drifts as in a dream around its mooring.

Later this morning we will pack up our gear, drive down to New Jersey, and on the next day, head home. I can't say with certainty that we should have come up here. There is such a strain now in these familiar and happy settings: the kids on the beach; the toddlers at dinner, mashing their food on their high chair trays. Even the lake itself — even now, this moment — seems more like a vast stillness than something alive that is really at peace.

I guess it's mostly by habit that we come to these places; and it is mostly by habit now — something dumb and animal — that we do many things, if we do at all. The swallow skims the water's surface, picking for bugs. I see an old woman out for an early morning row, catching her breath in a varnished guideboat, the sun on her oars like gleaming wings.

Maybe there is some kind of faith, or behind our habits some mulish hope that what once gave pleasure will give it again, though I'm sure in a very different way. For my daughter is dead, and she will never come back. She never saw these things or smelled this air. She never got to this place of her own making, never saw what love she left on the shore.

May 31

HYATTSVILLE

We are home, and things are all awhirl. Shopping and house cleaning. Beth, done with school for a time, is working in the garden, and I am replacing the pillars and railings on our back porch. Tomorrow, at noon, we are off again to the hospital where Beth is to have a hysterosalpingogram: a dye is injected into her uterus and followed on X ray to see if her fallopian tubes are still open.

So we are running around. Right now Beth is at the nursery buying impatiens to plant in the back beds and around Anna's tree. Soon I am heading for the hardware store for nails and moldings.

Beneath all this activity, though, runs a slow current of anxiety, not unlike what we were feeling at this time last year. We were waiting — for what we didn't know — and filling the time with our household chores, doctors' appointments, and the daily caring for Anna. Something was coming with the change into summer. And while we could never have imagined just what it would be, we could sense its weight in the leaf-laden oaks, and in the drone of the portable fans: one in our bedroom, and one in Anna's, churning the thick night air.

Once again I remember the smell of her hair, matted with sweat, and the feel of her room, as sweet and moist as a greenhouse. In her

174

sleep she began to creep or squiggle around in her crib: feet and knees and hips and elbows, pushing and wiggling, salamander style.

She must have been breathing by gills in that liquid air. Her hair would be sleeked, and often we would find her at the other end of the crib from where we had recently laid her down. Her head would be scrunched in the wet padded corner, her body still moving as if she was burrowing. What in the world could she have been dreaming? And where in her dreams did she think she was going, slithering like that, swimming almost, so deep into a softness?

By the end of May last year, she was turning over in her sleep, from her front to back. At first it would wake her up and scare her, but then in matter of days, it became a kind of amusement. On those mornings when she'd awaken us with her cooing, we would peek in her room and see her lying on her back, looking out toward her windows, and wriggling with wonder.

June 1

The hysterosalpingogram this afternoon showed that Beth's fallopian tubes are open. The dye filled the uterine cavity, then poured into the narrow tubes and out the ends through the fluted fimbria, fingered and funnel-shaped: the soft hands that catch the egg as it leaves the ovary.

So why are we having such trouble? Why isn't something happening?

June 2

Today is the first real summer day. Hot, muggy, the threat of afternoon thunderstorms. About midmorning I went out for a run without a shirt on, and now, a few hours later, I can still feel the heat on my back and shoulders. This is summer in Washington. The cloying air; the radios blaring on the street; the smooth skin wet in the creases. I know that this is the last month that Anna was truly alive.

And this — this smell and feel of the air, even with the roses blooming on the trellis and the lilies in the backyard budding — this was the season, too, of her death.

In the heat, we would have her dressed in one of those sleeveless and legless romper outfits that are still hanging in her closet. All that flesh was exposed, little folds at wrists, ankles, knees, and elbows. Holding her, your hands would catch in these places, the backs of hinges, soft and moist.

I was holding her like this one year ago today at a swim club of some friends of ours. It was hot and sunny. I was sweating in my plaid bathing trunks, and strands of Anna's hair had glued to her scalp. On the concrete edge of the wading pool, I sat with my feet in the cool water, and I thought that it would give Anna some pleasure if she could cool her feet as well. I remember holding her up and dancing her on the water, ankle deep, with that swaying motion that always made her smile. I was sure she would love it.

But no. First came that wide-open questioning look, and then the tears and cries, and the alarming blue tinge around her lips and nose. She cried and cried, and I remember holding her tightly wrapped in a towel and rocking her beside the picnic table until it was over.

It was not, by any means, one of her worst blue spells. We didn't even run for the oxygen tank that we had brought with us in the car, and ten minutes later she was gently asleep. Even so, those moments rattle like stones in the sieve of my memory. I think I was chastened some, and frightened anew. The unexpected violence of her response, and the threat of it, and the disparity between that and what I had construed for her in my mind — it surprises me even now. It bespeaks the other things that I have construed, that I have planned and thought that I had made sure of — those things that have never quite come to pass.

June 4

How could we have known or conceived on this day last year that a month later Anna would be dead? On that day we had brunch with some friends who have two daughters, five and seven years old. I sat

176

on their couch and put Anna in each of the children's arms, watching them rocking her, talking to her — two little girls making like mothers, and Anna, cranky as I recall, very much like an infant.

I would never have believed it then, and I hardly believe it today as I glance at her basket of toys beside the radiator behind me.

Yet I am not as tearful now as I was over those first weeks and months after she died. I am not visited every night by those images of her death. I think less often about "what she would be doing now," or what she would have looked like. So the pain, for me, has softened some; and I know that part of it, despite all *this*, is because I am simply forgetting. Things drift away. I can still feel her in my hands and arms, and smell her damp hair behind her ears. Yet her voice: I feel its heft, but the sound is vague, fuzzed. I worry that I wouldn't recognize it, wouldn't even turn my head, if I were to hear her calling somewhere.

And there, of course, is the problem. With the abatement of pain comes a loss of intimacy, a loss of vital memory, of seeing or hearing, smelling or touching. "Acceptance," "adjustment," "understanding," "peace," "healing" — everything I am supposed to be coming to — they are all euphemisms for these losses, for separation and letting go.

You quell pain by anesthesia. The drug slides in and the senses dull. But is the pain worse? Or is the loss of feeling? I simply do not know.

In the end, the only life is in the holding on, the feel of that, despite the inevitable letting go. Somewhere here are some intolerable truths: that what gives most pain can give most life; and what eases pain may give no comfort; and comfort, unalloyed, cannot exist at all.

What we are left with is the vigilance of our feelings, the hard clutch of a bare hand. This is not peace, nor comfort; but I think it is something, something even like joy. And that will have to do.

June 5

Our doctors have taken Beth off Pergonal this month because of her diminished response to it last month. So: no injections each night, no morning blood tests and sonograms. This month we go it alone, as it's always been done, as it was done with Anna, without assistance or surveillance.

About this time last year, we set up a playpen — it practically filled the living room — right around the corner from my study here. Though she wasn't crawling, Anna was wriggling more and more, kicking her legs, and while the Swyngomatic was still good for an hour or two of amusement, she seemed to want more space. So we'd lie her in the playpen among her toys. She had something called a Wiggleworm, which she would squeeze in three different places to make three different sounds: a high-pitched squeak, a rattle, a rustle. And then there was the clack of the bright plastic chains and ornaments that swung and clashed like garish jewelry from the Toy Bars above her head. She would bat at them and pull them, and spin a pyramid-shaped gadget with a mirror on one side, and on the others a clicking rabbit, sliding tabs, and a loud ratcheting dial.

Now what I am hearing are the sparrows quarreling outside my window and the cars slowing for the corner stop sign. At 3:15 this afternoon, the big school buses will rumble past, three in a row, as our house faintly shakes on its timbers. Soon I will hear the junior high kids roaring by on their skateboards, and then the children in our neighbor's backyard, playing beneath the flapping laundry.

Our neighbors behind us have five children, from elementary to high school age, all in a bungalow not much bigger than ours. They are wonderful kids, even when fighting, and in the summer with the windows open, their sounds carry over the chain link fence and up our new back stairs to our kitchen. One of them, Tom, is learning the saxophone, and in the evenings you can hear his awkward honking: "When the Saints Come Marching In." Another, Andy, is mad about bicycles, skidding them across the dirt. And their youngest, an eight-year-old, is an adopted girl from Korea, with thin legs, long black hair, and a soft fluty voice. Her name is Anna.

I am surprised that I haven't mentioned this before. Hardly a day goes by when one of us doesn't see her waving from her side of the fence, or running around their weedy yard, muddy-kneed, with her friends. Sometimes when I am working out in our own backyard, I will talk with her, and she will tell me in no uncertain terms what she likes and doesn't like about school. At other times she will surprise me by calling my name from her bedroom window, just to say hello, or "What are you doing?" as I am nailing up the balusters on our porch.

And then some nights we'll be sitting out on our back stairs, Beth and I, in the warm dusk with the trees heavy, the air still, and the back of their house but fifty feet away. Tom will have finished with the saxophone and the dishes will be done, their kids upstairs, the laundry in, and Kathy, the mother, will begin on the piano, something light and tendrilly, like a Chopin mazurka, washing across the chain linked yards. There will be stars squinting through the trees, and we will listen, enchanted, until she finishes playing or stops abruptly and calls her daughter's name. Upstairs we will see a shade pulled down, or a shadow move in a blue-curtained window; and then, one by one, their lights will go out.

June 6

Two evenings ago, while we were sitting on the back swing, we saw the first fireflies of the year, just a few of them, hovering above the grass, their amber lights blinking on and off. They reminded me of the fireflies that we saw last summer when were sitting out there with Anna. I don't know if she ever really saw them, though I do remember trying to hold her in such a way that her eyes would be aimed at a place where I thought a firefly would next appear. Largely I think I was unsuccessful, for no matter how I would aim her, Anna's eyes, intent on their own purpose, would always return to the dimming light way up in the trees. That is what *she* wanted to see.

Had she lived longer, I know there would have been more of these moments with me aiming her one way, and she turning her eyes toward the other. We would have had our little contests of will, and then some big ones. I have the feeling that there would have been battles — me yelling and she slamming her bedroom door. But I have

179

the feeling, too, that we would have lived and loved through it all, and found some awkward peace.

On summer evenings when I was a kid, my friends and I used to play wild games of badminton in my parents' backyard. Then, as the fireflies came out, or when the light dimmed so you couldn't see the birdie, we would stop the game, and still with all the sweat and frenzy of competition, we'd sprint around the yard with our flailing rackets, knocking fireflies out of the air. I am slightly disturbed to remember this activity now, the vicious boyish delight in exerting some measure of lethal power. And yet I must say, too, that I am still excited by it. For when you hit a firefly, the brittle wings and head of the bug will literally explode, leaving only the soft elliptic abdomen, about a half inch long, caught in the mesh of your racket. And if you strike the firefly at the moment it lights, then the abdomen, for some time thereafter, will steadily and magically glow on your racket. And if, in rapid succession, you hit another, and another . . . , your whole racket will be alight with them, and you'll wave it wildly around — their soft luminescence, right there in your hands, so long after the dying.

June 8

3:30 A.M.: Often I think that life is somewhat under control, and then I am suddenly up and sweating again with this fear, and I realize that in some strange way I am still scared for Anna.

What I couldn't get out of my head just now, as I lay in the hot breeze of the portable fan, were those couple of nights last summer, just about this time, when she would cry inconsolably, and we would madly walk her back and forth upstairs in the dark, and then hold her beside the humming oxygen concentrator in her room, with the end of the tube in the valley below her nose.

I remember my cold sweating, and the deep-down heaving of her crying, and the arching of her back. Should we call the doctors? The ambulance? Turn on the light and see how she looks. Better? Worse? How can you tell when you're squinting like crazy? When the light scares her, and the light scares us all? Well, maybe she'll nurse. Maybe that'll calm her. But she doesn't take. She is tinged with blue. Now all of us crying. Now walking her again. Rocking her and trying to keep the rhythm. Come on Anna. Jesus, Anna. Hold on. Come on. Easy, Snuggo, nice and easy. It'll be all right. It will. Believe me.

June 12

Last Friday evening, at a reception at the National Gallery where Beth is a volunteer docent, we ran into Dr. Palumbo, Anna's pediatrician. It was awkward at first, the jolt of it. Immediately, we all recognized one another — his sharp brown eyes and graying beard — but what do you talk to a pediatrician about when you're not in his office, and your child is no longer there in your arms?

Well, for a little while at least, we did talk about Anna, whom he clearly remembered. Over the course of four months, he and the pediatric nurses saw her once a week: weighed her, measured her, gave oral and injected antibiotics, and performed urine analyses.

I suppose Anna's doctors and nurses knew her better than anyone other than ourselves. They saw her wailing and smiling. They held her and slid in the urine catheters, shot in the needles, then rubbed her skin with the alcohol pad. And I suppose it was this sense of his firsthand knowledge that made me keep talking with Dr. Palumbo, asking him one question after another, as we stood in the crowded atrium beneath the slow-turning Calder.

In a way, I just wanted to hold him there for a while — hold everything still, and hold myself with him. He knew her. He knew us all. And for a mad instant, I had the urge to forcibly stop someone, to grab some stranger, anyone, it couldn't have mattered whom. I'd say, "Stop for a second and look at this man. Look hard at his face, and listen to what he will tell you. He was there. He knows. Look at those hands that held my child."

On the baby calendar here on my desk, Beth has noted some of the weights and measurements recorded by Dr. Palumbo and others during Anna's life. A full week-by-week accounting could be found in the hospital records; so much more of Anna's history could probably be uncovered there. But this is the real history, however incomplete: the records kept in Beth's own hand. These are Anna's weights and measures:

January 21, 1989 (at birth): 6.125 lbs
April 25 (at cardiac catheterization): 8.36 lbs, 21 inches
May 9: 9 lbs
May 16: 9 lbs, 22.25 inches
May 23: 9.5 lbs
May 30: 9.5 lbs
June 6: 9.5 lbs
June 13: 9.5 lbs
June 15: 9.7 lbs, 22.5 inches
June 20: 9.7 lbs
July 4 (at death): 17.2 lbs, 24.8 inches

If you were to plot this out on a graph (excepting her weight at death), you would see that for the most part Anna grew steadily, but slowly because of her heart condition. She was smaller than most children, and while we were aware of this, her comparative size was seldom of principal concern. If her heart could be mended, she would grow as any normal child. In the meantime, this was just the way that she was. It seemed wholly natural. Both Beth and I were smallish children and now are thin of build. For many years we had suspected that smallness is a sign of delicacy, refinement, charm, etcetera. Now, of course, we were sure of it.

June 15

We have been in an accident — shaken up, but we are all right, including Jessie, who was lying on the backseat. Yesterday, about 3:30 P.M., we were going southbound on Route 95, about ten miles north of Baltimore. Beth was driving. At the bottom of a hill, she had to slow abruptly for merging traffic, and a speeding tractor-trailer plowed into us from the rear, smashing us forward into the car ahead, which in turn was propelled into the car ahead of it. Remarkably, no one was hurt. None of the cars were thrown into oncoming lanes of traffic. There was no fire; no ambulance even was necessary. Still, we are trembling slightly. This is the closest call we have had, and it is hard to say what we are thinking about it.

Mostly, right now, I am just remembering. As soon as Beth hit the brakes, I looked back through the rear window and saw the big grill of the truck coming at us, with "International" written on the chrome. I saw blue smoke around the tires. I remember saying, "He's going to hit us!" — and that was all. It didn't occur to me that "this could be it." Nor was I afraid. Nor did my life pass before my eyes; nor, in that instant (and I actually regret this) did I think of Anna. I simply knew that he would hit us. Hard. Straight on. Nothing came to me that was remotely profound, moving, or insightful. What filled my head was just a pure, dumb, physical fact.

When the sound ended, there was a moment of quiet. And then Beth was screaming, and I was afraid, and I was just trying to hold her and tell her, probably screaming myself, that we were all right. I must have said it ten times, over and over — what I realize now were the same words I repeated to Anna (and as much to myself) on those nights we held her when she was turning blue. Or later, on those days and nights almost a year ago, when she lay in the hospital, all changed and different and dying. I just kept saying that it was all right. It would be all right — as if by saying it and saying it again, I could make it so.

On the radio and TV these days, the airwaves are filled with ads for events on the Fourth of July. Sales. Celebrations. Barbecues and fireworks displays. This year will be the biggest and best. The lowest prices, the best deals. The sky, they say, will explode with light.

June 17

10:30 P.M.: Father's Day. And we spent the afternoon and evening gardening in the backyard, just as we did last year. At the nursery we bought two shrubs; and home again, I dug the holes, we mixed dirt and peat moss, then put the plants in the ground. Such is the shape of our defiance now. These are the barricades; these are the weapons: a sack of mulch on a rusted wheelbarrow, a spade sunk to the hilt.

We do these things of a year ago, and we remember these things of a year ago. Our lives are there in the upturned dirt and in the mixing in of the new. Childless, we remain her parents, and I am her father still. There is a strange joy in this small defiance. In the plunge of the shovel and the leap of the soil. In the grit that holds beneath our nails.

Last night we slept at a friend's house, where we were baby-sitting their two kids. Their house is about a hundred yards from the railroad tracks, where I often hear those long freight trains when I am awake in the middle of the night. From their bedroom, you can hear the engines coming from many miles away, a slow gathering of sound, a high hum that deepens until it roars right outside the window, all light and combustion; then fades, humming, utterly gone — leaving only the dark rumble of wheels, and the mirror on the bureau faintly trembling.

June 18

On June 15 last year, we took Anna to the Georgetown University Developmental Evaluation Clinic for a follow-up exam. Because of all her congenital anomalies and corrective surgeries, Anna's development was to be closely monitored during her childhood. That particular morning was warm and sunny with wide shafts of light coming through the windows of a yellow room with red mats on the floor and children's toys and gadgets all around. Anna was in her pink rompers, and with all these new things to see, she was wildly alert, wired, as we took turns holding her.

It was one of those mornings when everything must have been right with her. She just babbled, squealed, smiled, and wriggled. And as I think of this, I feel again that swelling pride that I felt as the various specialists came in, one at a time, and examined her, held her, babbled with her, put her in this position and that, and gave her toys to rattle or little problems to solve. I remember Beth holding her in her lap at a low children's table while Anna searched for a red ball hidden beneath a plastic cup. Then, in a tiny soundproof chamber with a speaker on either wall, I held her as different noises filled the room, and Beth and a doctor watched through a dark window. Twice Beth's voice came from one speaker and then from the other. "Anna? Hello Anna. Pumpkin pie."

I wish you could have held my daughter then. I wish you could have felt her jump at a sound.

All of this took up most of the morning, and by the end, it was clear by the doctors' responses that despite her problems, Anna was doing quite well. We made another appointment for September 28, when Anna would be through her heart surgery and she would be eight months old. In the meantime, they said, we should be comforted by her progress. Mentally she seemed to be right on the ball, and her motor development, while slowed — she was about a month behind — was more than acceptable, given her condition.

June 19

So we were elated. Anna was "doing very well," and here was the confirmation, like a just reward. Of course we were anxious about her surgery scheduled for late in July, but on that afternoon at least, it seemed suddenly distant, just another hurdle on her way to full health. It was one of those times when we could let a vision of her life, and ours, unfold before us: the times in the hospital, yes; but also the trips to Piseco, the mad games of tennis, canoeing, the stories that we would tell.

I know that in my exuberance I was less cautious and reasonable than Beth. I knew the danger, yet I thought that in the end Anna could do just about anything; that given what she had been through and how she had fought, survived, and flourished — I thought that nothing in the world could stop her.

In fact, I actually had it in mind to take her up to a ball game in

Baltimore in the next few days. The Yankees, my childhood team, were in for a weekend series. We could all go to a night game when it would be cool. Beth could nurse Anna under a poncho. We'd bring the small portable oxygen tank in case of blue spells. And the Yankees — this was the part that seemed most farfetched — might even get some decent pitching.

Need I say that Beth was less enthralled by my vision than I, and the next evening I drove to Memorial Stadium with a friend, a recent father himself — his son, a second child, had been born in early May. As luck (or Beth's clairvoyance) would have it, it rained, and during a fifty-minute delay, we sat under an umbrella, he and I, passing the time. We talked about baseball, and we talked about paternity, about our fears and excitement for our children's futures. I remember I was all wound up about this, blathering away. But it wasn't until Anna's memorial service last July 8, that this same friend, speaking over the cries of his own infant son, reminded me of something I had mentioned that night as the rain came down. I said, "I do not look forward to the day when Anna loses her innocence." And by that I meant that I regretted the day when she would come to know the cruelty and devastation and unfairness in all of our lives.

But now, today. To think of that time when I had imagined and hoped and feared for her future, when I had dared to fear for her loss of innocence.

And to think, too, that within three weeks she would lose all chance of losing her innocence. That she would die innocent and unknowing; and it would be all of us who would lose our innocence, all over and over again.

So as I think of the rain falling in the lights and pooling on the wide blue tarpaulin that night, I feel all of my old fear and hope, and at the same time I feel the terrific distance between then and now. Again I know that there is no comfort when a child dies, even when a child dies in innocence, and perhaps with no awareness of evil or death. It is still a total loss. She is not here. There is air in the place where she should be, and a cup of ashes to fill our hands.

It is no better to die young than it is to die when youth is lost. If Anna had lived to lose her innocence, she might also have lived to gain in love.

June 20

At the end of last July, some weeks after Anna's death, we received in the mail a warm note of sympathy from the developmental pediatrician who had examined Anna, and with it he sent our copy of the summary of her evaluation. It is in dry, rather uninspiring prose, but as I read it now, just as I read it then, I am filled with more than I can say. These doctors saw Anna. She was there. And this, in part, is what they found.

Anna turns over. She can grab at objects. She lifts her head when she is on her stomach. When she is pulled to sit she has head lag. Anna makes cooing noises. Anna is very social and outgoing.

Growth Parameters	NCHS Percentiles
Length: 22½ in.	5th
Weight: 9 lbs, 13 ozs.	5th
Head Circumference: 40 cm	10th-25th
Weight for Length Ratio:	50th

Anna's growth is considered small but proportional for her size. Her neurological examination reveals her primitive reflexes are mature. Automatic reactions are developing.

Overall Impression: Anna is 4 months, 24 days and she is doing very nicely. Her developmental skills are appropriate for her age. She was born with multiple congenital anomalies consistent with the Vater Syndrome. Her medical condition has been stable and she has appropriate intervention planned with upcoming surgery to correct her congenital heart disease.

Anna's strengths are her nice vocalizations and excellent social responses. Anna has slightly low muscle tone, but this is consistent with a child with congenital heart disease.

Recommendations: We would like to see Anna back at 8 months of age. There are no specific developmental concerns at this time so there is no need for any additional therapeutic input.

I know that from the outside, this may not seem like much: a dry list of characteristics. Yet for me they bring back certain small things: like the way she could sit now with just a little support, your hand lightly across her back. Or the way she would smile at perfect strangers. Or if you held her and wagged your head at her, or blew your breath through her hair: how she would squint and giggle. That was my child.

June 21

I realize that I have been avoiding this, putting it off, just as I was trying not to see it last year: the slow, subtle, and inevitable worsening of Anna's heart condition, even as she grew and giggled and smiled. For the most part, she was so happy. She gave you every reason to fasten onto her potential, to look beyond the danger, though of course it was there. If you look closely at the later photos, you will see it: the joy and the danger in the same face. Even as she spins a toy or sucks both her thumbs, her eyes all huge and bright; even then you will detect a certain paleness in her skin, and a faint bluish tinge in the curve above her nose.

I have mentioned that on every Tuesday, we would take Anna to the cardiologists' office at the hospital where she would have an EKG, an oxygen saturation test, and her doctor — it was Dr. Beder then — would examine her and listen to her heart with a stethoscope.

On June 20, we had another one of these appointments, and while nothing else was unusual, Dr. Beder seemed to spend more time listening with the stethoscope, moving the flat end of it, like a silver dollar, here and there on Anna's chest. For a moment he stopped while we settled Anna, who, by now, was getting cranky. He listened again as if to make sure of what he had heard, then pulled the arms of the stethoscope away from his ears and let them fall down around his neck. He said, "The murmur she has — it sounds a little softer." He didn't seem terribly concerned. He said he'd like to run a blood test.

Of course I'll never know exactly what he heard, though I trust his ears and his judgment absolutely. Still I wonder: what do you hear when a heart sounds softer? What had become of that wild swooshing sound, that sound with the sea in it, that I had heard a few months before?

I wish I had asked him if I could borrow his stethoscope and listen to her heart myself. Perhaps the waves were less peaked, the wind less lashing, the troughs a little more shallow. But the sea in her heart — it must have been there, lulled, gathering, a sound still with heft and life. For I know that it raged before it stilled. I heard its pulse in my ears.

June 22

From the cardiologists' examination room, we went straight to the lab where Anna's blood was taken to be tested: another needle in her foot, the sudden wrench of her crying, the blue in her face, and the dark blood drawn out. On the next day, the day that Anna was five months old, my parents arrived, midway on a trip from New Jersey to North Carolina. On the following morning, exactly a year ago today, I was back at the lab with my mother, whose own blood was drawn to be screened and cross-matched with Anna's.

Then my parents continued on their trip; and that evening, after Anna was in her crib, and while I was in the kitchen and Beth was downstairs with the laundry, the phone rang and I picked it up. It was Dr. Beder, who said he had been unable to reach us during the day. He said he had the results of Anna's blood test. He said that her hemoglobin level had risen quite rapidly, that this was not an emergency, but that this result, in conjunction with the softened sound of Anna's heart, meant that her pulmonary stenosis had progressed more rapidly than they had anticipated. Soon her body would need more than her heart could give her. Soon the threat of waiting would exceed the threat of intervening. She was reaching that point, and now, quite soon, it would be time.

I asked him if he was sure, and he said that he had spoken with

Dr. Hopkins. They had reviewed her case and the recent results, and they were in agreement. If it was all right with us, they would schedule her surgery for six days later, at 9:00 A.M. on June 28. She would be admitted on the day before.

I don't recall exactly what I said on the phone at that point, though I must have said yes, all right, with that pang of resignation that I can feel right now.

What I mostly remember is going down the basement stairs with the monitor in my hand, and Anna's breath in the monitor as if she was breathing in my hand, and then seeing Beth standing beside the washing machine in her crazy black shorts, the ones with the ice cream cones embroidered on the front and back. She was holding some soiled sheets in her arms.

I told her that it was Dr. Beder on the phone, and I told her what he had said. I think I remember the sheets falling out of her arms and piling on the concrete floor. And I know I remember the white fear that gathered in her face — I have seen it since, and she has seen it in my face as well. I remember exactly what she said. She said, "No. They can't take her. We're not ready. Not now. Not yet."

June 24

If you were to walk down to our basement and stand at the bottom of the stairs as I have done just now, you would see my table saw to your right with the pile of sawdust beneath it, and behind that the dusty workbench with tools strewn around, scraps of lumber, and on the shelves the screws and nails in labeled glass jars. To the left and a little behind stands the ironing board, Beth's sewing machine, and from an overhead wire among the pipes and cobwebs hang some skirts and shirts and pants. Along the wall to the left are shelves of camping gear, the vacuum cleaner, dryer, washing machine, and double sink. As I write this, the washing machine is rhythmically churning. You can smell bleach and sawdust, just as I could smell it on that evening as I stood there last year. And it was mixed, then, with the sharp sweet smell of Beth's hair after a warm summer's day.

We were beside the washing machine, holding each other, and I was trying to be calm and reassuring in that way that I do when there is little reason to be calm or assured. I repeated the obvious: that so far Anna's care had been magnificent, that we had gotten the best doctors that we could find so that now we could trust their judgment.

But none of this seemed to matter to Beth. She seemed to know some things at another level. We weren't ready for this. Things were happening too fast, too out of control. As she has mentioned a few times in the year since, it was then, that evening, with the sheets on the floor and the machine churning, as we leaned against one another and I tried to explain — it was then that she first sensed that Anna would die.

I know we called our parents sometime that evening, though beyond that my memory is hazy. What I see is all in my imagination, and yet it could very well have happened this way: I see us shutting off the lights and going back up the basement stairs. I see us going through the kitchen and dining room and turning up the narrow stairs to the second floor. I see us going into Anna's room, with the street-lamp flickering behind the feathery pin oak, and the impatiens pressed up against the screens. I hear the fan whirring in the doorway and the cars on the road outside. The air is dim and thick with Anna's breath and sweat. She is sleeping in the way that she always slept: on her stomach, head to the side, thumb in mouth or thereabouts, knees scrunched up beneath her.

I see us standing there with our hands at our sides, saying nothing, then leaving her room, the door open, and coming back down the creaking stairs.

We are children more than we like to admit. First Beth, then I: we called our parents and asked them to come.

Just as we have asked them to come, again, this year.

June 25

Now near the bottom of our basement stairs, straight ahead against the cinder block wall, stand the boxed-up playpen, the car seat, and the Swyngomatic with its legs folded up, the chair tilted back and furred with dust, the nylon belt unfastened.

How my calm and assurance — however feigned, however real — how it mocks me now. Yesterday when I came up the basement stairs, I went out on the back porch where I have finished building the new balusters and railing. Out over the railing, I saw the orange lilies along the garage. I saw the bench-swing in the corner with the mildewed roses climbing the lattice. Along the fence, I saw Anna's tree, which ruffled like a skirt in the breeze. It was green and flourishing; it has grown half a foot, though this year at least, it will not blossom. On the clothesline Beth had hung out the sheets to dry in the sun. It was a spectacular day, a crisp windy Sunday morning, and the white sheets — they seemed to be running like steeds.

What does all of this mean? Anna's death? Our lives since? Almost a year later, I haven't a clue. Little holds in my hand that doesn't slide through my fingers, squirting away the harder I grasp.

Today Beth says that she can feel her period coming. Bloating, cramping. Things drift and mingle, but they do not hold; and again what might have been will be washed away.

As I come toward an ending, I wish we could come to some kind of balance. I wish I knew of some compensation, something just or right, as I understand it. That would be nice, some sense of closure. And perhaps that will come, though frankly I doubt it. For I know of nothing that can right the death of a child — even the birth of another. That would be good. That would be wonderful. It would give our love a place to live. But it would not replace what is lost. It would not return to Anna what should have been hers.

Sometimes we think we are being taunted, or used, or punished, or just made fun of. And then sometimes we even think we have been strangely blessed ever to have had Anna in our lives. But mostly now I think that it is all beyond us — if there is anything at all beyond. Perhaps in the end there are no big meanings, no truths, nothing that will stay fixed in our palms. And what we are left with is mostly the grasping, the holding hard until letting go, or the doing of something to keep the hands moving, like the hammering in of a stake that bears no apparent sign or direction. It bears mostly the mark of its own hammering. The point is buried. The exposed end is mashed and flattened. It means something here was held and hammered. Something here. Unfinished. Done.

June 26

In those few days right before we took Anna into the hospital, I don't think we did anything very strange or different. I recall a slow-building pressure, a sense that something was coming, a hard, trying time, but for me at least there was as yet no terrible urgency, no believable sense — how could I have believed it? — that these were among the last days when she would be alive. I remember canceling a workshop that I was to teach on the Wednesday night of her surgery, though I felt reasonably sure that we could continue the class on the following week. Otherwise, Beth and I went ahead with the things we had already planned. On the night of the 24th, a Saturday, we had some friends here for an early dinner, and I remember their three-month-old son sleeping in Anna's stroller as Anna slept in her bassinet beside the dining room radiator. On the following morning, we had brunch with some other friends while their daughter crawled around on our floors. That evening I picked up Beth's mother at the airport; her father was overseas on business; and then the next day, the 26th, my parents arrived.

It was on that afternoon, a year ago today, that I went with my mother to the hospital, to the lab's "Specimen Collection Area," where she lay in her crisp white blouse and navy blue skirt, with her arm straight out, and her blood running through a tube and into the plastic bag with Anna's name typed on the label.

It was also on that afternoon that Beth's mother took all those photos of Anna, eight of them: two when she was napping upstairs in her crib, and a series of six as she was cooing and kicking, and grabbing at toys in her playpen. In them, you can tell that Beth has just washed Anna's hair, for it is straight and long and combed back behind her ears. She is wearing that pink sunsuit that shows all of her arms and legs. She is happy. In some of the photos she is looking up, smiling, and wriggling with something that someone has said. I can't really describe her eyes, except to say again that they were large, dark, almond-shaped like Beth's, and they were all alive.

June 27

On this day we took Anna into the hospital. It was the last full day that she would be conscious. It was also the day when Beth's sister Ann, after whom Anna was named, gave birth to her first child, Libby, a daughter.

On the morning of this day last year I baked popovers for breakfast, and we took four more photos, two with Anna on my father's shoulder, then two more with her in Beth's arms. In the latter two, Beth is holding Anna beside the refrigerator. They are both in their nightclothes, and Anna's hair is ridiculously wild. The last photo is the one where Anna is looking right at the camera, big-eyed, surprised, her mouth part open. This is the one that Beth would clip on the refrigerator eight weeks later — it is hanging there now — the one that I saw one morning when I came downstairs about the time that I began keeping this journal.

We left for the hospital in the early afternoon, a little rushed, for we had originally been told to arrive at 2:00. But at noon we got a call requesting that we come earlier because the doctors, in addition to setting up the IV antibiotics that day, would try to get a urine catheter in place.

So off we went. And even now in the corner of Anna's closet, there is the maroon nylon diaper bag, filled with the things that we packed that day: four diapers, two receiving blankets, two pacifiers, wipes, one colostomy bag, and the white sweater my mother had knitted.

June 29

That was where the writing stopped two days ago, and though I sat here trying all yesterday morning, the anniversary of her surgery, it wouldn't continue. I had thought I might bring all this to an end by telling the story of Anna's last week, day by day, event by event, just as I have tried to tell her story thus far. But I find now, when I most want to keep writing, that I can't write — or at least not in that vein.

Right now, the writing of this — as much as I depend on it, and as much as I want to do it — it seems beyond me. There is so much that I seem unable to say, or I am too confused to say, or too sad.

How can you do justice to a single life? How can any mountain of words touch a thing like that?

The last entry on our baby's calendar is June 28, 1989. In Beth's writing, it says, "9 A.M. Anna has surgery." After that, the days are blank, white boxes without any words, without even numbers. Nothing.

So where do you go from a place like that? How do your days of words come to an end? And how, in the end, can they possibly matter?

July 1

Yesterday I didn't attempt to sit down here, even with all that happened on these days last year. Instead, we spent the entire day in the yard, digging holes and planting shrubs around the back porch, both of us covered with sweat, dirt, and peat moss.

Perhaps it was my having given up for a short time, or perhaps it would have happened anyhow, but early this morning I dreamed of Anna for the first time. It was so shocking and vivid. I woke up sweating and weeping and wondering.

In the dream I was on a train, in an old dusty passenger car with wicker seats and spinning overhead fans. It was a troop train of some sort, and we were trundling through desolate countryside in Turkey, though I have no idea how I knew that. In any case, I was sitting alone

195

on a wicker seat on the right-hand side of the aisle. I didn't feel I was one of the troops, or that I was connected with anyone else on the train. What I felt was a keen sense that I was in a strange place, tired, unclean, and that I had been away for a very long time.

It was then that I saw Anna standing about three seats up on the left-hand side of the aisle. It was simply her, undoubtedly. The same hair, ears, nose, eyes; her mouth the same, except for a row of small bottom teeth, a few of them twisted, and for an instant that bothered me. She wore a clean white shirt, navy blue corduroy overalls, and white leather shoes. She had one hand on the seat beside her. She was looking right at me, and though she didn't say anything, she was smiling in that impish way of hers; she knew exactly who I was, and I knew exactly who she was.

I said her name. I said, Anna. And then she let go of the seat, and with the train rocking her about, she awkwardly walked, arms out to her sides, fingers splayed, duck-walked as toddlers do, across the aisle toward where I was sitting.

But even as this was happening, with her hair blowing and eyes all dark and wide, I knew, too, that this wasn't actually happening. This wasn't quite right, quite real, because I knew, even as she came closer and closer, I knew that she was dead.

In the dream, I never scooped her up in my arms or touched her with my hands. I moved over on the edge of my seat, and bending down, I put my face beside her face, where I could smell her hair, and where, on leaning a little closer, without actually seeing her now, I could just touch her face with the side of my face: cheek, temple, and the damp place where her hair began.

July 2 and 3

These days have moved so slowly, the nights so still and humid. I have just put the air conditioners in the windows upstairs, and now you can hear them buzzing. The house is closed up, cool, and stale. The ceiling fan whirls above me. Outside the grass is turning brown;

leaves droop; and the afternoon air, all gray and swollen, smells of thunderstorms.

I am reminded these days of how long it was, that time last year: how little we know of our lives' last lashings, the mysterious rallies and mysterious descents; how strong life is when it's held so hard.

What I have of that last week are mostly fragments, some of which I have mentioned before. This, in part, is how it happened:

It is midnight in the hospital, a slot of light beneath the door, and I am lying on one of the rollaway beds where we will sleep in Anna's room. I am watching Anna nurse for the last time before her surgery. I see the IV tube running down from the pole and into a place in her hair. I hear the sounds and I smell the milk. I see Beth's face in the dim light, and the peculiar tilt of her head, sideways and down, almost as if it is bowed.

Beyond the light, the nurses' shoes squelch in the hall. Trolleys rattle and then subside. I see Beth's long hand around Anna's bottom. I see Anna's long fingers open and close, clench and release, breathing it seems as she sucks.

Now in a blue-tiled room without any windows. On the bottom floor. Surgery. In the hall: people on gurneys. People around us in scrubs, going this way and that in their powder blue pants, slipper things, and powder blue hats like shower caps. They leave us for a time, and we hold Anna there. Rock her. Bounce her. Lift her up where she giggles on the coming down. She is all alive in this hard-gleaming room. Eyes. Smile. The tuning-fork hum of her morning mood.

And the surgical assistants are back with the syringe and the anesthetic. They are Maggie, from Mary, and Debbie Devine — names with a strange soothing. They could be mothers themselves, or will be sometime soon. They coo and smile and touch Anna's hair that is squirting out at the temples. They will know her heart with their freckled hands. They will be with her until the end.

Anna is in my lap when they shoot in the syringe, and we are both holding her with our hands. She is a happy child, looking all around, when her eyes soften and close.

The rug in the waiting area is blue and stained. Yellow and orange Naugahyde chairs. A crucifix on the wall, phones on the other wall. People are smoking — even here, around the corner from Cardiac Intensive Care. I am turning the pages of Chekhov's "A Dreary Story," remembering more than reading: an old and eminent professor of medicine, an insomniac now, is approaching his death, weighing up the waste of his life.

We all jump when the phone rings, and how can you not overhear? Bypass. Angioplasty. And some people talk, they have to talk. A fundamentalist minister with a string tie. Or the parents of a sixteen-year-old boy. "He was fine just a week ago." Some kind of procedure, and now an aneurysm, everything different. Brain. Heart.

I cannot look at their eyes.

We take turns taking walks to escape the smoke. Lunch in the cafeteria, then Beth to the milk bank to pump her breasts, to keep up the supply for when Anna will nurse again.

Seven hours pass and the phone rings. It is four in the afternoon. It is Maggie's voice, and all has gone well; Anna's heart repaired, and we will see her soon.

In the small bright room with the wide window, with the sound of machines and smell of machines, she seems to float on the white sheets, face up, arms out, like someone asleep in a pool. Her face is the color of skin in moonlight, her hands open and upturned. She is puffy, but it is her. She smells different, but it is her. There are tubes and wires, but it is her. A machine breathes, but it is her. You speak her name, and it is her. She closes her hand on your finger.

A priest is standing in her doorway when we arrive in the early morning. In his hands he holds a small open book, and in his mouth are sounds that I do not understand.

She is worse. The morning sun streams in the window. Gleaming jets fly over the trees. Her whole body is swollen, transformed, her skin so taut beneath your lips, the lids of her eyes like tops of mushrooms, bulging, shut. The words of the doctors are "oliguric," "edema," "ascites." Her kidneys not working, her capillaries leaking, her body drowning in fluid that she cannot expel. They are trying diuretics, the most powerful diuretics. All day we watch a plastic cup where the red rubber urine catheter drains. Doctors fill the room. A drop. A drop. When a slight trickle comes, we actually cheer. But it slows to a drop. It doesn't come.

At night, we walk on P Street, on the slick bricks beneath the damp and drooping magnolias. Pee, Anna, pee. But it doesn't come.

Still she closes her hand around your finger. Still you speak in the swollen funnel of her ear. She seems to sleep in a place where the snow is falling, where the fine snow ticks on the branches, falling and falling and muffling the road.

But wherever she is, she seems to know. She seems to hear. She closes her hand on your finger.

In Conference Room A, down the hall from Cardiac Intensive Care, there is a blackboard on the front wall and X-ray viewers, like opaque windows, along the back and sides. We push aside the chairs and set up roll-away beds. First two. Then four. Because our mothers will stay, they need to stay: to mind their children who mind their child.

From home, they bring food and clothes. I drink Coke like an addict. At night we lie on the rollaway beds. The chest X-ray machines rumble in the hall; the square of light shines in the door. Then it's out for a moment. Or was it an hour? And where have we been? Where is she?

The time before dawn is almost quiet in her room. Two nurses, a resident. Slouched in chairs, groggy-eyed, watching the monitors: peaks and troughs across a screen, the flashing green and red digital readouts. There are hushed voices outside the door. Doctors glide in and out. The lights are dimmed, the window dark. And always the slow heft of the respirator, like an old man breathing in sleep.

We hold Anna's hand, talk into her ear, and softly, with the dawn, Beth begins to sing: the lullabyes that I have heard in Anna's room, or in the bath, or long ago on the lips of my own mother, on the lips of all of our mothers.

> *A cherry when it's bloomin', it has no stone.*
> *A chicken when it's pippin', it has no bone.*
> *The story of my love will never end.*
> *A baby, when it's sleepin', has no cryin'.*

A nurse gives me a small tube of ointment, and I squeeze some onto my finger. I rub it onto the lids of Anna's eyes, too swollen now to open. It will keep her skin moist and pliable. It will soothe her pain. It will help her to live somehow.

In the orange light of the new-risen sun, the lids of her eyes are slick and gleaming, hard like porcelain. She has a fever; her weight has doubled; no fluid expelled; her blood pressure slides. And still her hand closes over your finger. It does.

Dopamine. Dobutamine. Norepinephrine. Furosemide. Sodium bicarbonate. I read the words on the IV pumps that are lined on the table beside her crib. Each has a tube feeding into the tube that feeds into the catheter in Anna's arm. There is a tube in her mouth. There are drains in the sides of her chest, plastic tubes that drip into bags that hang from the sides of the crib. And there are wires to sensors on top of her chest, and there are tiny wires that disappear, like threads, beneath the dressing over her heart.

I look at all this and I look at her, and what I feel beyond everything else is a pride, raw and wild. We bring our mothers in to see her. We tape photos of her on the head of her crib: at home in her swing, with that mischievous smile.

I want to say to anyone who will listen: look, look here, look at this. I am as proud as I was on the day she was born — all red and shining. Otter hair.

There is something here that we do not understand.

We are talking in the conference room with Dr. Hopkins. His voice is deep, plain-spoken, and he folds his big hands in front of him. Despite all the preoperative antibiotics, Anna has the symptoms of septic shock, a massive infection. And yet her blood tests are negative, and she isn't responding to more antibiotics.

He simply can't say exactly what is happening, though she seems to be fighting hard. Her mended heart is strong and pumping. She is not giving up. No one is giving up. If it is all right with us, he would like to put a passive dialysis machine in the femoral artery of her right leg. In the long run, it might stunt the growth of her leg, or worse, she might lose part of her leg; but in the meantime, it should remove some excess fluid. It might give her some time, and a chance to recover.

Now he looks at his hands, and he looks again at us. And what I see in his drawn face is all of his fatherhood. I see his own children in their various ailments, large and small. I see the ragged edge of what he knows and what he can hold, and what, perhaps, can only be hoped for.

He stands again at her crib with his white coat on his sloped shoulders. He adjusts the rates of the IV pumps, studies the monitors and studies her.

And now it feels as if we are coming to a place like the end of the land, where the thin-frozen lake lips over the sand, and where we must crawl, and spread our weight, and feel gently before us with only our hands.

The passive dialysis machine is like a fancy filter in the fuel line of a car, and for hours we watch the slow drops of fluid drawn off, as her bloated leg goes gray and purple. Now I smell the blood that fills her colostomy bag. She is bleeding inside. Her temperature dips. They set up heat lamps, and she floats in the orange light, dawn and dusk, day and night. Her window changes, but not her room. The dialyzer removes less fluid than she is taking in. She is huge, all different. And now the monitors surge and plummet. The doctors talk and talk in the hall, and the nurses' hearts are in their eyes. They touch our arms and they touch our shoulders.

We rub the ointment on Anna's eyelids, and they gleam and gleam in the light. When you say her name, she squeezes your finger, and what you feel in your hand will not let go.

It is midnight, or thereabouts, though the time hardly seems to matter. Again we sit in the conference room with Dr. Hopkins, while our mothers wait in the hall. He is tired, drained. The days and nights have oozed one into another, and now he shakes his head. Frankly, he says, he doesn't know how Anna lives, how she fights, though surely, with her gaining fluid like this, she cannot go on for long. Still he is not giving up. He has an idea that he has discussed with his colleagues, at best a fifty-fifty chance. It is a procedure that has never been done at this hospital before, or perhaps anywhere else.

He would like to remove the passive dialysis machine, and using the same vessels in her leg, put her on an ECMO (a heart-lung) machine with a dialyzing unit added to the system. If it works, it will allow excess fluid to be drawn more quickly from her blood. It might buy her some more time in which she still might recover.

At 3:00 A.M. we are sitting beside the nurse's station across the hall from Anna's room. Over the white counters and commuter monitors, we see the orange light in her doorway, and the doctors and technicians surrounding her bed, assembling the new machine. Their eyes are intent, their voices low and succinct. Down the hall, the lights have been dimmed, and through a window, we see the streetlamps behind the hospital, and the darkness that is the courtyard, the lacrosse field, the distant trees, and the space above the river where the blinking jets are gone.

It is the time of night when the physical therapists do their work. We hear it from open doorways of dark rooms: a slow strange cantoring sound, a sound with depth and roundness. The therapists are

202

clearing the lungs of cardiac patients, drumming their backs with cupped hands. The sound fills the halls and fills our ears. Those hands on skin stretched over a hollowness. You feel their weight in your bones.

In the hall we talk again with Dr. Hopkins. He looks us straight in the eye. Anna is on the ECMO machine, but it's not helping her enough. The flow rates are not as high as he wanted; there is congestion in her lungs; and now she seems to be spiraling down. He has done all he can do. He hasn't given up hope, but now he has no more answers. What is left, he says, is for us to be with her. What is left he just doesn't know.

When we go back in her room, there is the big machine, but we do not see it now. There is only Anna in the orange light, her arms outstretched, palms up, the white sheet pulled to her neck. In the lamps, her eyebrows are almost transparent, and the tips of her hair have begun to bleach, as if, all night, she's been out in the sun.

As another dawn comes, there is a kind of reverence in this small room as the city awakens. The doctors are gone; the door is shut. The effusionist monitors the ECMO machine, and the nurses stand quietly behind us.

We sit on stools, craning over the bed, and we say those things that you say to kids. Dumb things. Silly things. Nicknames and nonsense words. We sing and we say hold on, and in my hand I feel her holding. It is as though all of her life has poured into her hands. And all of our lives have poured into our hands — all that is wild and willed, twined and untwined, and twined again.

We are in a hospital, in a room that pulses with medical equipment, and yet we seem to be beyond the medicine now, in a place where there is only a window, a bed, and there is Anna.

It is all in her hands, but she does not let go. The planes glint in the sky, and she does not let go. The sun rises out of the window, and still she does not let go.

203

And then, as from a dream, I hear an odd bustling. The nurses are moving excitedly and pointing at the screens, and the effusionist stands, saying, "Look! My God. Look at this!"

The nurse — it is Jodie — opens the door, and one by one the doctors return. Their eyes are wide when they look at the monitors. Her heart rate is up, her blood pressure up, oxygen saturation is up, and slowly the flow rates increase, allowing the machine to remove fluid from her body, more than she is taking on.

There is something here that we do not understand, something beyond us all. Dr. Hopkins leans over the bed with his hands on the chrome bar, and for a while, he is just looking at her — I don't know what he is thinking. Then I see him straighten and walk to the window, where his back is turned and he seems to stare out at the distant trees and sky. But in the mirror above the sink beside him, I see the side of his face reflected. I see his graying hair and the loose skin that rides on his collar. I see a man grown old and humble with the wonder of decay, and the wonder of healing, and the wonder of what he can never know. I see beneath his bushy brows that his eyelids are red and closed.

I am running in the midday sun, but I barely feel the heat. I am flying up and down hills, past fancy townhouses, parks, stores, and restaurants with cosy courtyards. There is light banging off windshields and chrome. Horns blast. Smells of tar, hamburgers, boxwood, and perfume. There are people in shorts and bright shirts. People watering gardens, walking dogs, taking out trash, and bringing in mail. People laughing, arguing, pushing strollers or handtrucks. People eating on checked tablecloths, sleeping on benches, playing guitars, singing, sighing, bent over books, maps, making love behind louvered shutters, out of this blinding sun.

"Go on. Get some exercise. It looks like she's holding her own."

And I am running without even feeling my legs, running with possibility. I could run all the way home to Hyattsville, past our house with the yews out front and the white boxes in the dormer windows. And behind the clumps of impatiens, behind the screen and the tieback curtains, I'd see her head propped on Beth's shoulder. I could see them rocking there.

There is the faint blue light before another dawn. Beth, exhausted, is down the hall, asleep in the conference room; I am sitting on the stool beside Anna's bed; and the intensivist has just come in and shut off the overhead lights and heat lamps. The blue dawn fills the room and washes over her sheets. It glints on a small silver flashlight that the intensivist holds in his hand. He says that Anna's swelling has gone down to the point where he might be able to open her eyes. I say I'd like to stay and see; I'd like to help if I could. So he flicks on the flashlight and shines it on Anna's face. Slowly he pushes open her left eyelid while shining the light directly into her eye.

And it is like no eye that I have ever seen. For a moment, he turns the flashlight away, then passes the beam quickly across her eye. But nothing moves, nothing changes. Her iris so thin, her pupil so wide. It is like looking through glass or clearest ice, down and down, and into a stillness.

With my index finger I push open her other eyelid, her skin and lashes greasy with ointment. He shines the flashlight, and it is just the same. He turns off the flashlight, and there is an instant of black, a blazing horror, and the milky light leaks back in the room.

Beth sleeps on the rollaway bed with her denim skirt fanned across her legs. Her eyes are closed, her breath lightly lapping. In her face there is only a distance, as if all has been released, or quelled, leaving a vast calm.

How do I wake her to what I have seen? How do I wake her to what I am fearing? She turns in her sleep like a slow swimmer. Is it cowardice or consideration? It is probably both: I go out the door without disturbing her, and go back into Anna's room.

Out on the courtyard between the buildings, the afternoon sun skates on the flagstone, wavering the thick air. There is a plot of grass here, marigolds, a wooden bench, but mostly we lean against the low brick wall. Six floors above is the window of Anna's room where she lies with a metal band screwed tight to her skull — they are doing an ultrasound of her brain.

Beyond the wall, we look out on the familiar lacrosse field, the trees, and the silvery planes above the river. In the last few hours, there must have been a change of wind, a change in the usual takeoff and landing patterns, for the jets now are climbing over the water, tilting upward, full-throttle, peeling off to the north and west. They come one after another, like boxcars at a crossing, filled with passengers heading home for the Fourth of July. The planes rip through the same slot in the sky, time and again without even a scar — just threads of smoke in the sun.

The sonography is negative for intracranial bleeding or excess fluid, and never has Anna's brain been without sufficient oxygen: so we are all assuming the best. Just look at her. The swelling is down. Her eyelids soft. Touch her here, or here. Cheeks, brows, narrow lips — she is coming back to who she was. You feel the bone beneath her skin.

Yes? What?

I am jostled from sleep. It is Beth's hand, Beth's voice, but there is something in both that I cannot wake to. It is deep in the night. Beth has been sitting up with Anna while I have lain down to sleep in the conference room. Now her body is shivering, and her voice is shivering. "I had to wake you. You have to come." Suddenly Anna's heart is beating irregularly. Her blood pressure down, the monitors going crazy. In a whirl of activity she floats on the white sheets, everything spiraling down. We crane over her bed and sing.

Before the dawn Dr. Hopkins arrives, his face gray and unshaven. He looks at Anna and studies the charts and wobbling lines on the monitors. He talks with the staff, and back in the conference room, he will speak once more with us. He closes the door behind him. We sit in chairs beside the smudgy blackboard. Before he says what we already know — before he says what we cannot believe — he lays open his wide hands.

It has the feel of an early holiday morning. It is Independence Day. The streets and sidewalks are empty. People are sleeping late. In a slow ellipse, a single jogger goes round the lacrosse field while the big sun, furry with haze, rises out of the trees. Through the window it fills the small room with an orange hue, eerie and autumnal. And in that light my daughter lies, a beautiful thing, almost as she was born. Her eyelids gleam. Her hands are clenched. Our words are filling her ears.

Now the door is shut; the doctors gone; the nurses — Jodie and Sharon — stand behind us. In Anna's face there is neither peace nor pain. And there is no change, no movement, no sense, right then, of a threshold crossed, or anything recognizable that is actually happening. There is only her presence — I feel it now — and Jodie's hand on each of our shoulders, as light as the first fall leaves.

July 4

Today, one year later, our parents again are with us, and it feels good to have them here. This morning I made waffles, and then we drove to Takoma Park to watch the big parade. After lunch we all went to the hospital and up to Pediatric Cardiac Intensive Care, where we donated another book, *Barnyard Families*, to the Child Life Room that was furnished, in part, with money from Anna's memorial fund. Once more Jodie was on duty — on the same day, on the same shift as when she had laid her hands on our shoulders. Today, though, standing in that room, we chatted about the new cardiac unit, and who among Anna's nurses and doctors were still there — almost all of them, it seemed.

Soon after we came home, we heard a soft knock at the front door. I got up, opened it, and there was Anna, the daughter of our backyard neighbors, standing demurely behind the screen. Her straight black hair, perfectly parted, fell halfway down her back. In her hands she was holding a thick cellophane-wrapped coffee cake, as if she was afraid to drop it.

I asked her to come in, but she said no thank you; she had to go home. Then holding out the cake, she said, "This is for you. And Beth too."

I took it from her, and thanking her, I could see the thin moon-shaped slices of apple arranged on the top, glazed with sugar and smelling of cinnamon.

She said, "My mother and I just baked it."

"It's beautiful," I said.

We stood there awkwardly, until she lifted her hands and let them fall against the sides of her legs. "Well, see you."

I watched her hurry back down the stairs, all willow-limbed and hair flowing. Then I turned and brought the cake into our house, feeling its warmth in my hands.

ABOUT MIDNIGHT

We have just come back from the Mall downtown, where we sat with a picnic on the west lawn of the Capitol and watched the fireworks out over the Washington Monument. It is an impressive sight, even at such a distance: those big blossoms of color, and then the concussion, a second later, that you feel deep in your chest.

Now I have taken the dog out and locked up the house. Out in the yard there were still a few fireflies — it's been an unusual year for them. I've never seen them in the day; I can't find them in the bushes or hiding in the grass. But on these warm, moist, summer evenings, when we are out in the yard at dusk, they rise out of the grass around us, hundreds strong, all flash and dazzle, like bright rain going upward. I haven't seen anything like it, even as a kid in my parents' backyard. They are so thick, so many. And they have such small and delicate wings — to lift up so much light.

August 7

Yesterday, a year, one month, and two days after Anna's death, we went to the hospital where she was born, cared for, and died, and we found that Beth once again is pregnant.

This pregnancy, our doctor says, may be difficult and complicated — there are so many things that we do not know. But we are as filled now with hope as we are filled with the sadness for what has been lost.

Last night about 10:30 when I came home from jogging, I sat on the swing in the corner of our backyard where so often we would sit with Anna. I heard the birds ruffling in the oaks and the neighbors' fans whirring in their dark bedroom windows. I smelled the day's heat rising from the grass, and saw, without surprise, Anna's tree beside the fence, standing in its wavering pool of shade.

Against the gray back of our house, I saw the pale porch balusters and railing that I had built and we had painted a month or so ago. Then, from the bathroom window on the second floor, came the sound of the shower running. I saw the light behind the beige curtains, and in my mind I could see the water sleeking Beth's hair, streaming over the slow curve of her stomach and the whitish scar of Anna's birth, and pooling now in her hands.

All that was alive we cannot hold, and all that can become we cannot know. But this, at least, is remembered. This, for now, is said. I feel in my chest Anna's wild heart; I hear those trumpeter swans. Sitting out on the swing, I see the stars through the shimmering leaves. And with a jolt I realize that the fireflies are gone — gone from the air and gone from the earth — though I do not, I will not, forget their light.

Postscript

March 27, 1992

There are, of course, no simple happy endings, though there are the most extraordinary and happy additions. Our second daughter, Emma, was born on April 22, 1991, at Georgetown University Hospital. She was born healthy, her light blonde hair matted to her scalp, her eyes almost as big as her sister's eyes, and they were wide open, bright, like headlights emerging from a long tunnel. Most of Anna's doctors and nurses were at the hospital that day, and many of them came by to say hello, and to hold a new life in their arms.

As with Anna's birth, there was our excitement, pride, the shock of Emma's otherness — but the shock, too, of how different she was from Anna. Though we had known all along it couldn't be so, and we had reminded ourselves over and over, at some level we still must have believed that in this new birth Anna might somehow be reborn, that what had died might be regained. But of course Emma arrived as her own distinctive person: a little heavier, longer, more lean than Anna, and as I say, she was blonde, like her father. As we held Emma during those first moments after her birth, we were drained, overjoyed, and suddenly in tears. For we knew then that lost lives are not reborn, that

211

this, here, was a whole new wonder, a different wonder. And this was how it must be.

Emma is a healthy, beautiful, delightful child. She has two small teeth in the bottom of her mouth. Her hair flows over her collar. She crawls like a marine and stands when you hold her fingers, which are long, even longer than Anna's. Once again our house is filled with babble. There is a smile when you come in the door. Toys, many of them Anna's, cover the rugs; bits of food harden beneath the high chair; diapers ripen in the hamper. It is spring again, and outside my window I see the daffodils blooming beside the leggy yellow forsythia. Out back Anna's tree is swelling at the tips, as is Emma's tree, another dogwood that we planted shortly after her birth.

As for Beth and me, we are splitting time caring for Emma, and still teaching and writing, our usual jobs. On Anna's birthday and on the Fourth of July, we all go over to the hospital, where we donate a few books and then talk with some of Anna's nurses. It is a ritual for us now. At home again and after Emma is asleep, I light the candle on the dining room table. Beth gets the album, Anna's album, and the package of loose photographs. We put in a few more, as many as we dare. We say the things that we remember, the things that are in our bones. Soon I blow out the candle, Beth shuts off the lights, and we go upstairs.

Last week in our kitchen, Beth was carrying Emma in her arms when Emma reached out toward the refrigerator. We have another refrigerator now — the old one quit — but taped on its front is that same old photo of Anna where she, too, is in Beth's arms, with her eyes huge and her hair all windy and wild. It was toward this photo that Emma reached out her hand. And while I am aware that at this stage she grabs at almost everything, and while I know she didn't know just what she was doing, still I am moved to think of Emma reaching out for her sister's image. For someday she will do this again, and someday she will want and need to know. Someday she will look hard and straight at Anna's face, and we will tell her what we remember about her sister, and what happened, and what we all have gained and lost.

Now Emma is napping in the dormer room upstairs where Anna used to sleep. On my desk is the monitor, and I listen for her rustling sounds, her whimper and cry as she wakes. If I need reassurance — if I need to know that I am alive — I can go up there and, standing by her door, I can hear her soft liquid breath, in and out, like waves on a lake at dusk. Then I can go around the corner into our bedroom and take from my bureau the small blue box, undo the pink ribbon that Beth has tied there, and once more hold Anna's ashes in my hand.

I can touch the ashes while I hear the breathing. I can feel the needle that pains and heals, that mends but leaves the scar.

I touch the ashes and hear the breathing. Both I can hold in my heart.